Econometrics for
Daily Lives

Econometrics for Daily Lives

Volume I

Tam Bang Vu

BEP BUSINESS EXPERT PRESS

Econometrics for Daily Lives, Volume I

Copyright © Business Expert Press, LLC, 2018.

First published in 2018 by
Business Expert Press, LLC
222 East 46th Street, New York, NY 10017
www.businessexpertpress.com

ISBN-13: 978-1-63157-686-7 (paperback)
ISBN-13: 978-1-63157-687-4 (e-book)

Business Expert Press Economics Collection

Collection ISSN: 2163-761X (print)
Collection ISSN: 2163-7628 (electronic)

Cover and interior design by Exeter Premedia Services Private Ltd., Chennai, India

First edition: 2018

10 9 8 7 6 5 4 3 2 1

Printed in the United States of America.

Abstract

A number of everyday problems faced by you and your loved ones can be solved by collecting data and then analyzing the relationships among different factors. This textbook will help you perform data analyses to understand these relationships.

This volume, Volume One, starts with easy and fun models to help you gradually familiarize yourself with the subject. Part I, comprising three chapters, introduces elementary topics in econometrics. Chapter 1 reviews basic statistics and primer Excel operations. Chapter 2 offers the first linear model of simple regression analysis. Chapter 3 extends the model to multiple regressions.

Part II, also comprising three chapters, guides you into intermediate topics in econometrics. Chapter 4 discusses modeling issues and regression problems in cross-sectional data. Chapter 5 analyzes three simple dynamic models for time-series data. Chapter 6 introduces panel data and simple techniques to handle this type of data.

Keywords

business, data analysis, econometrics, economics, Excel

Contents

Preface

If you think econometrics is boring, think again. Econometrics can be enjoyable if you focus less on the abstract theory of the subject and more on the applied topics so that you can solve your everyday problems.

For example, you might wish to know the relationship between the cost of buying a house in your hometown versus renting the same house so that you can decide whether to buy or to rent. You might also wish to know how increasing prices of certain goods affects the revenue of your company. This textbook will help you analyze these relations. The book is written for first-year MBA students, upper-division undergraduate students, businesspersons, and other readers who wish to apply econometric concepts to improve their lots in everyday activities.

An Applied Approach to Econometrics

The focus of this textbook is Applied Econometrics, so the only prerequisites for the course are high school statistics and college algebra. The book is not an intimidating 400- to 600-page textbook. The theoretical sections are made easy by discussing only the concepts that are required to conduct basic data analyses. This enables the text to be quite informative while consisting of only two volumes of less than 150 pages each, both of which can be easily covered in one trimester or one semester.

To make the book more accessible, Microsoft Excel is the only econometric package required to perform all applications in the book. Two supplementary folders are provided. The first folder is named Data Analyses and contains all text and Excel files that accompany the Data Analyses sections in this book. The second folder, Data for Exercise, comprises all data for the exercises in the text.

A third folder, Answers to Exercises, will be provided to instructors after a book order is received.

Topics in This Textbook

This book discusses most of the econometric methods frequently used in practice. Volume One introduces elementary and intermediate-level topics such as simple linear regressions, multiples linear regressions, ordinary least squares, generalized least squares, cross-sectional data, simple time-series techniques, and panel data analysis. Volume Two discusses several advanced topics and applied issues in econometrics such as non-linear forms, instrumental variables, advanced time-series techniques, simultaneous equation estimations, limited dependent variables, regression discontinuity analysis, and difference-in-difference estimations.

The Fictional Characters in This Book

A team of professors and classmates is introduced in this textbook to provide you with an enjoyable learning experience.

The professors:

Professor Empirie is an empirical researcher. She teaches all Data Analyses sections in this class.

Professor Metric is a theoretical econometrician. He is responsible for explaining any theoretical concept in this class.

The professors guide you step by step through the chapters while providing plenty of daily-life examples to make the theoretical concepts easy to understand.

The Students:

(i) Touro works for a tour-guide company called Tourista.
(ii) Booka is the owner of an online bookstore called Bookwebki.
(iii) Taila works for a tailoring shop called Tailorie.
(iv) Invo works for an investment company called Investos.

The students show you how they apply their knowledge of econometrics into solving various problems in their daily lives.

Acknowledgments

I wish to send a big thank-you to Dr. Jeff Edwards of the Business Expert Press (BEP), who has been a driving force behind this book.

Many thanks go to several former students of the University of Hawaii, who are now my colleagues. Special thanks to Jeffrey Pieper, my former MA student in the China-U.S. Relations Program, who went over details of my writings and to students from my Econometrics classes, especially Roy Thompson, who read my first draft carefully and gave valuable comments on technical aspects of the book.

Thanks as well to Exeter and its editing team members for their help with editing and formatting of this book.

I also wish to recognize help, updated information, or comments from Drs. Philip Romero, Scott Isenberg, Sheri Dean, and Charlene Kronstedt. The support provided by these individuals in their respective roles has been crucial to the successful completion of this book.

PART I

Elementary Topics

This part contains three chapters:

CHAPTER 1

Introduction

"It is a normal distribution!!" exclaims Booka, the owner of Bookwebki. Invo the investor is curious, "What is that?" Booka replies, "I tried to draw a histogram of my store's sales on a type of book with different designs, and it came up very close to a normal distribution." We all look at the teacher, "What is a histogram?" Professor Metric, our teacher, responds cheerfully that we will learn these basic concepts very soon and that by the time we finish this chapter, we will be able to do the following:

1. Discuss the nature of an econometric model.
2. Explain basic concepts of probability.
3. Distinguish inferential statistics from descriptive statistics.
4. Perform simple data manipulations and calculations using Excel.

He then leads us into the first section of the lecture.

What Is Econometrics?

Econometrics is a branch of economics that uses statistical methods and mathematics to estimate any relationship in everyday life, test any hypothesis and theory, evaluate business strategies, and implement public policies. There is a big difference between a theoretical model and an econometric model. A theoretical model studies hypothetical relations between variables using a general function. For example, let the variable WAGE represent the average weekly wage of a person and the variable SPEND represent his or her spending on nondurable goods and services such as food, clothes, haircuts, and so on. Then we can write a theoretical model as

$$SPEND = a_1 + a_2 \, WAGE, \qquad (1.1)$$

where a_1 is a constant representing the average nondurable spending by a person with WAGE = 0, and a_2 is the change in spending due to a unit change in personal wage.

An econometric model quantifies that relationship. In order for you to estimate the value of the parameters a's and test for their significance, the model is written in a particular way as follows:

$$SPEND = a_1 + a_2 \, WAGE + e, \qquad (1.2)$$

where a_1 is the intercept and a_2 is the slope of the regression line. The random error, e, accounts for a set of unobserved factors that might affect SPEND other than WAGE or any random component in the model. Figure 1.1 illustrates this relationship, with a_1 as the intercept, a_2 as the slope of the regression line, and e as the distance from an actual data point to the regression line.

The variable on the left-hand side is called the dependent variable (SPEND in this case), and the variable on the right-hand side is called the independent variable if we have only one variable on the right-hand side (WAGE in this case) or explanatory variables if we have more than one variable on the right-hand side.

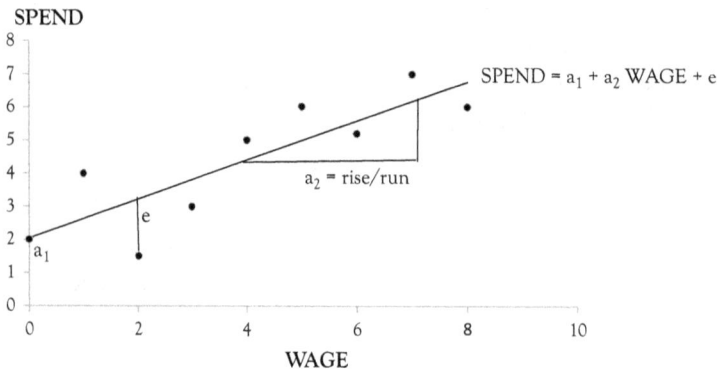

Figure 1.1 *Relationship between wage and spending*

Basic Steps

There are usually three basic steps in econometric research:

Step 1: Selecting the Model

Depending on the problem and the availability of the information, an appropriate model should be decided. In the preceding example, our model is specified in Equation (1.2).

Step 2: Collecting and Analyzing Data

Data can be collected directly by the user (primary data) or by someone other than the user (secondary data). Data analyses consist of constructing data plots, obtaining descriptive statistics, and performing certain techniques to quantify the relationship between a dependent variable and one or more explanatory variables.

Step 3: Interpreting the Results

Evaluations of the results are performed based on hypothesis testing and other measures. Based on the interpretations of the results, implications concerning economic theory and practical policies are drawn.

Statistics Primer

Professor Metric emphasizes that statistics provides important tools for data analysis and you can spend your whole life studying it. However, some basic knowledge of statistics, discussed in the following section, is enough to understand econometric techniques in part one. More concepts will be introduced later.

Probability

Probability is the likelihood of an event occurring and is measured by the ratio of the chosen case to the total number of possible cases. At this moment, Professor Metric offers the class a basket that contains 24 balls identical in size, except that twelve are rainbow colored, six are red, four are green, and two are blue. We learn that each group of balls is called a category.

Table 1.1 Frequency distributions of the balls

Category	Absolute frequency	Relative frequency
Blue balls	2	2/24 = 1/12
Green balls	4	4/24 = 1/6
Rainbow balls	12	12/24 = 1/2
Red balls	6	6/24 = 1/4

At this point, Taila the tailor says, "Oh… I love the rainbow ones." So, Professor Metric tells her, "Let variable X_1 equal getting a rainbow ball, then the possibility of getting a rainbow ball if you are allowed to pick just once is called the probability of X equals X_1 and is written as

$$P(X_1) = 12/24 = 1/2.$$

This probability is also the relative frequency of the rainbow-ball category whereas the number of rainbow balls is the absolute frequency."

Professor Metric continues that if we let Y_1 be the probability of getting a green ball, then $P(Y_1) = 4/24 = 1/6$, which is also the relative frequency of the green-ball category. We follow his instruction and put all frequencies into a frequency distribution table (Table 1.1).

The probability of getting a rainbow ball or a green ball in one pick is

$$P(X_1 \text{ or } Y_1) = (1/2) + (1/6) = (3/6) + (1/6) = 4/6 = 2/3.$$

If one is allowed to pick twice with the rainbow ball returned to the basket after the first pick, then the probability of getting a rainbow ball twice is:

$$P(X_1 \text{ and } X_1) = (1/2) \times (1/2) = 1/4.$$

Professor Metric tells us that sometimes, we encounter a joint distribution, such as the percentage of Native Hawaiian males who graduated from high school. He shows us Table 1.2, which lists the joint distribution of high school graduates in Honolulu in 2000 by race and gender.

The table shows that the percentage of male Native Hawaiian high school graduates is $P(Y = 1, X = 1) = 0.11$, whereas that of female Native

Table 1.2 Joint distribution of high school graduates in Honolulu

	Native Hawaiian (Y = 1)	Non-Native (Y = 0)	Total
Male (X = 1)	0.11	0.38	0.49
Female (X = 0)	0.12	0.39	0.51
Total	0.23	0.77	1.00

Hawaiian high school graduates is $P(Y = 1, X = 0) = 0.12$. Further, percentage of male non-Hawaiian high school graduates is $P(Y = 1, X = 0) = 0.38$ and that of non-Hawaiian female graduates is $P(Y = 0, X = 0) = 0.39$.

Professor Metric says that this concept will be very helpful in the later chapters when we learn to estimate effects of certain explanatory variables with different demographic characteristics; for example, wage differences between male workers who live in New York and female workers who live in South Carolina.

Descriptive Statistics

Statistics is divided into descriptive statistics and inferential statistics. Descriptive statistics organizes a dataset into useful forms such as summarizing tables, charts, graphs, and relevant measures of the underlying data. Inferential statistics generalizes the characteristics of a population, which is the whole body of a group, by examining its samples, which are subsets of that population.

Professor Metric says that the two aspects of descriptive statistics that are most important to econometric study are measures of central tendency and measures of dispersion.

Measures of Central Tendency

Central tendency is related mainly with the mean, the median, and the mode. The mean of a population X with N observations is called the expectation of the population, $E(X)$, which is the weighted average of all Xs with the weight $P(X = X_i)$, where $i = 1, 2, \ldots, N$.

$$E(X) = P(X_1) * X_1 + P(X_2) * X_2 + \ldots + P(X_N) * X_N \qquad (1.3)$$

Statisticians usually assign a Greek letter to any parameter of a population, and $E(X)$ is assigned the letter μ_x (read as "mu-x"). Professor Metric reminds us that for a given population, there is only one $E(X)$. In contrast, there are many samples. The average of a sample with N observations is notated as $\overline{X}$, and the formula for calculating this sample mean is:

$$\overline{X} = \frac{1}{N} \sum_{i=1}^{N} X_i \qquad (1.4)$$

From Equation (1.4) we can determine that the sample mean depends on the sample size. The larger the sample size, the closer the sample mean to the population mean. This is called the Law of Large Numbers (LLN). Also, let a be a constant, then

$$E(aX) = a * E(X) \qquad (1.5)$$

Professor Metric reminds us that the median is the value of the middle observation, where 50 percent of observations in the underlying dataset have values smaller than the median and the remaining 50 percent have values greater than the median. For example, given a dataset 1, 3, 2, 5, 4, 6, 7, 3, 8, we can sort the data from the lowest value to the highest value as 1, 2, 3, 3, 4, 5, 6, 7, 8, so the median is number 4.

The mode is the value that occurs most frequently. In the aforementioned example, the mode is number 3.

Measures of Dispersion

Variance measures the variability of the data. The population variance of X is the weighted average of the squared deviations from the population mean, in which the positive and negative deviations receive equal weight. Hence, the variance is also said to measure the dispersion of a distribution, and the population variance is:

$$Var(X) = E[X - E(X)]^2 \qquad (1.6)$$

This variance is assigned the Greek notation σ_x^2 (read as sigma-squared-x). Booka then asks, "Why do we have to square the deviations?" Invo offers an anecdote as a way of explanation, "My friend and I were playing basketball in his backyard. My first throw was roughly six inches to the left of the basket, and the second one was roughly six inches to the right. My friend applauded, 'You got it, on average of course.'"

We all laugh. Professor Metric says, "Exactly, if you do not square the deviations, then their average is zero because some values are negative and some are positive, so there is no dispersion." He then says that the sample variance of a particular sample with N observations can be written as

$$s_x^2 = \frac{1}{N} \sum_{i=1}^{N} \left(X_i - \bar{X} \right)^2.$$
(1.7)

Touro the tour guide points out that he often sees the sample variance expressed as

$$s_x^2 = \frac{1}{N-1} \sum_{i=1}^{N} \left(X_i - \bar{X} \right)^2$$
(1.8)

Professor Metric says that Touro's remark is true because the preceding formula turns out to be a biased estimator of the population variance, so in practice, many econometricians use the second formula to calculate the sample variance. He also says that given a constant c,

$$Var(cX) = c^2 Var(X).$$
(1.9)

The formula for the covariance of two populations is easy to understand because all we have to do is to enter Y in place of another X in Equation (1.6). And thus, the covariance of X and Y measures the linear association between them.

$$Cov(X, Y) = E\{[(X - E(X)][Y - E(Y)]\},$$

$$Var(X + Y) = Var(X) + Var(Y) + Cov(X, Y).$$
(1.10)

However, if X and Y are independent or not correlated linearly, then

$$Var(X + Y) = Var(X) + Var(Y).$$
(1.11)

Since the formula for variance requires that we square the deviations from the mean, the squared deviations become very large and hardly measure the true dispersion. Hence, the square root of the population variance, called the population standard deviation, σ_x, and its sample counterpart, called sample standard deviation, s_x, is usually used in descriptive statistics.

Professor Metric says that descriptive statistics are useful, because a researcher can have an understanding of the underlying data before making any inference about the population by employing inferential statistics, the basic concepts of which we are about to learn.

Inferential Statistics

Inferential statistics aims at drawing conclusions on the characteristics of a population through repeated sampling. Drawing the first random sample from a population will yield some information about the population. Drawing another random sample from the same population yields somewhat different results. Each sample has a mean value, as shown in Equation (1.4). If we draw many samples from a population, then the average of those sample means is the expectation of the sample mean.

$$E\left(\overline{X}\right) = E\left(\frac{1}{N}\sum_{i=1}^{N} X_i\right), \tag{1.12}$$

where $E(\overline{X})$ is an unbiased estimator of $E(X)$ when we draw an infinite amount of random samples.

Booka suddenly says, "I forget what the difference between an estimator and an estimate is?" Invo offers an explanation, "An estimator is any rule or formula related to the data and is used to estimate the population parameters, whereas an estimate is a particular value once we follow the rule or substitute the estimated parameter into the formula."

Professor Metric praises Invo for his correct answer and continues, "The unbiasedness property of the sample mean is written as:

$$E\left(\overline{X}\right) = \frac{1}{N}\sum_{i=1}^{N} E\left(X_i\right) = \frac{1}{N}\left[N * E\left(X_i\right)\right] = \mathrm{E}\left(X_i\right) \tag{1.13}$$

While the sample average in one sample might be greater than the population expectation, that in another sample will be less than the population expectation. An unbiased estimator implies that in repeated sampling, they will average out to zero." We also learn that this unbiasedness, which comes from repeated sampling, is completely different from the LLN mentioned in the section on descriptive statistics. The LLN implies that the sample mean approaches the population mean when the sample size approaches the population size. The unbiasedness of the sample mean holds for any sample size as long as we draw infinitely many random samples from the population.

The repeated sampling process yields various values of $\bar{X}$ and so has its own dispersion called the sampling variance.

$$Var\left(\bar{X}\right) = Var\left[\frac{1}{N}\sum_{i=1}^{N}X_i\right] \tag{1.14}$$

Because random sampling guarantees that the observations in a sample are statistically independent of each other, we can apply the property in Equation (1.11), where the variance of a sum equals the sum of their variance. In addition, since each X_i is from the same population, we can make the assumption that each draw has the same variance σ_X^2. Hence, a combination of Equations (1.9), (1.11), and (1.14) and this assumption yields:

$$Var\left(\bar{X}\right) = \frac{1}{N^2}\sum_{i=1}^{N}\sigma_X^2 = \frac{N\sigma_X^2}{N^2} = \frac{\sigma_X^2}{N} \tag{1.15}$$

The standard deviation of the sample mean is called the standard error (*se*):

$$se = \sqrt{\frac{\sigma_X^2}{N}} = \frac{\sigma_X}{\sqrt{N}} \tag{1.16}$$

Since σ_x is unknown, the estimated standard error is:

$$Estimated\ se = \frac{s_X}{\sqrt{N}} \tag{1.17}$$

where s_x comes from the square root of the sample variance in Equation (1.8). In practice, most researchers drop the word "estimated" and simply call the expression in Equation (1.17) the "standard error." Regardless of this terminology, we all understand that it is an estimated value.

Professor Metric concludes the theoretical section with a summary of the important concepts and reminds the class to read the next section, which will be taught by Professor Empirie.

Data Analyses

Professor Empirie starts with basic data manipulations in Excel.

Working with Data

First, we need to install a tool to perform data analysis.

Add-In Tools

For Microsoft Office (MO) 1997 to 2003:

> Click Data Tools on the Tool Bar, then choose Add-Ins from the drop-down menu.
> Choose Analysis ToolPak from the new drop-down menu, then click OK.
> When you want to use this tool, click Data Tools and then Analysis ToolPak.

For MO 2007 or 2010:

> Click the Office logo in MO 2007 or the File tab in MO 2010.
> Click Options in the menu.
> Choose Add-Ins at the bottom of the left column in Excel Options.
> The Add-Ins window will appear; click on Go at the bottom center.
> Check the Analysis ToolPak box in the new dialog box and then click OK.
> When you want to use this tool, click Data and then Data Analysis on the Ribbon.

Column Chart Versus Histogram

A column chart is often used for qualitative data because it displays categories on the horizontal axis and the absolute frequency or relative frequency on the vertical axis. On the contrary, a histogram is good for quantitative data because it displays classes on the horizontal axis (e.g., price ranges) and the frequency (or relative frequency) on the vertical axis (e.g., numbers of goods sold for each price range). Professor Empirie tells us to go to file *Ch01.Fig.1.2* in the folder Data Analyses.

We learn to draw a column chart (Figure 1.2) for the absolute frequency distribution of the balls in Professor Metric's example on probability distribution by following these commands:

Select any chart type you wish to use; for example, clicking on the first choice gives you the chart in Figure 1.2.

Professor Empirie says that drawing the relative frequency distribution yields similar shapes as those in Figure 1.2 and that we can see more chart drawings in Vu (2015).

Booka offers the dataset on music books from her store so that we can learn to draw the histogram that she tried earlier in the class. Because the dataset is too long to display, we all go to the data in the file

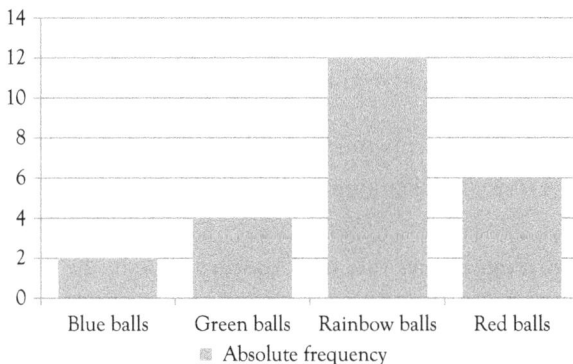

Figure 1.2 Column chart for the absolute frequency distribution

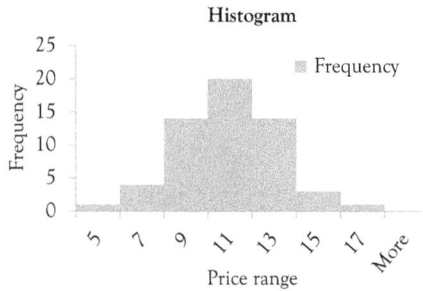

Figure 1.3 Histogram based on book demand

Ch01.Fig.1.3 and proceed to draw this histogram using the following commands:

> Go to Data on the ribbon and click Data Analysis.
> A dialog box appears.
> Choose Histogram and click OK.
> Type B1:B58 into the Input Range.
> Type A1:A8 into the Bin Range.
> Check the box Labels.
> Click the button Output Range and type D1 in the box.
> Check the box Chart Output and then click OK.
> To reduce or eliminate the spaces between columns, right-click on a column.
> Choose Format Data Series in the drop-down menu.
> A dialog box appears.
> Move the indicator on the No Gap line to the left as much as you wish, then click Close.
> The histogram is displayed in Figure 1.3.

Invo recalls Booka's comment at the beginning of the class and points out that it is true: The distribution of book sales is very close to a normal distribution.

Professor Empirie says that the frequency table in the data file looks narrow and long. It will look better if we transpose the table to a horizontal arrangement. We will perform the following steps:

> Copy cells D1 through F9 and then right-click cell D16.
> Under Paste Options choose Paste Special.

A dialog box appears.
Choose Transpose and click OK.

The frequency distribution in horizontal style is shown in Table 1.3.

We all turn to Booka and ask, "So how about interpreting the results?" Booka says that the first four classes are of music books in paperback. The very first class has books that cost at least $5.00 (represented by number 5 in the first cell) and contain only music scores in black and white. The second class contains the books costing from $5.01 to $7.00 (represented by number 7 in the second cell) and each book comes with a black-and-white portrait of the composer. The third one includes books priced between $7.01 and $9.00; books in this class come with color portraits. The fourth one consists of the books costing from $9.01 to $11.00 and brief biographies of the composers. The last three classes represent the hardcover counterparts of the first three. Based on the information in Figure 1.3 and Table 1.3, Booka can now fill up her inventory by placing an order from a supply chain according to her customers' demand.

Importing Data

Professor Empirie says that we can create a dataset by sending out survey forms and entering the results into an Excel spreadsheet. This is called a primary dataset. If we use data collected by other people, then we have secondary data, which sometimes comes in a text-delimited format with observations separated by spaces or commas. The file Ch01_text in the folder Data Analysis is in this format. To import the data to Excel, we need to follow these steps:

Open a blank Excel file and click on File at the top-left corner of the ribbon.

Table 1.3 Frequency distribution of book demand

Price range	5	7	9	11	13	15	17	More
Frequency	1	4	14	20	14	3	1	0

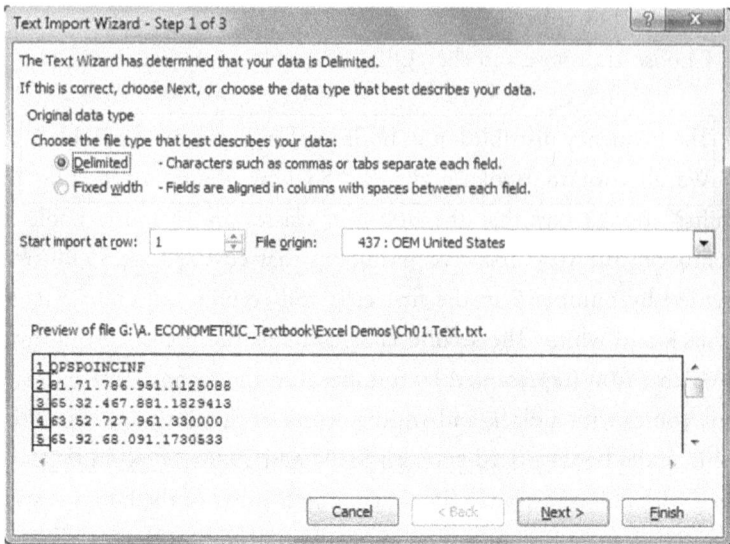

Figure 1.4 First text wizard dialog box

Click Open and then double-click the folder Data Analysis.

In the Open window look for the bottom-right box labeled All Excel Files.

Use the arrow to change the selection from All Excel Files to All Files.

Double-click the file Ch01_text.

The first Text Wizard dialog box appears as in Figure 1.4.

In this dialog box, check the button Delimited if it has not been checked and then click Next.

The second Text Wizard dialog box appears as in Figure 1.5.

Check the box Tab because the observations are separated by spaces in this case (if observations are separated by commas, then check the box Comma).

Most of the time, this is all we need to import the data, so click Finish.

The data are now in Excel format, ready for you to perform data analysis.

To save this dataset, click the arrow in the box Save as type.

Choose either Excel Workbook or Excel 97–2003 Workbook and click Save.

You can save with any name you wish to.

In this textbook, the file is saved in the folder Data for Exercise as *Demand_US*.

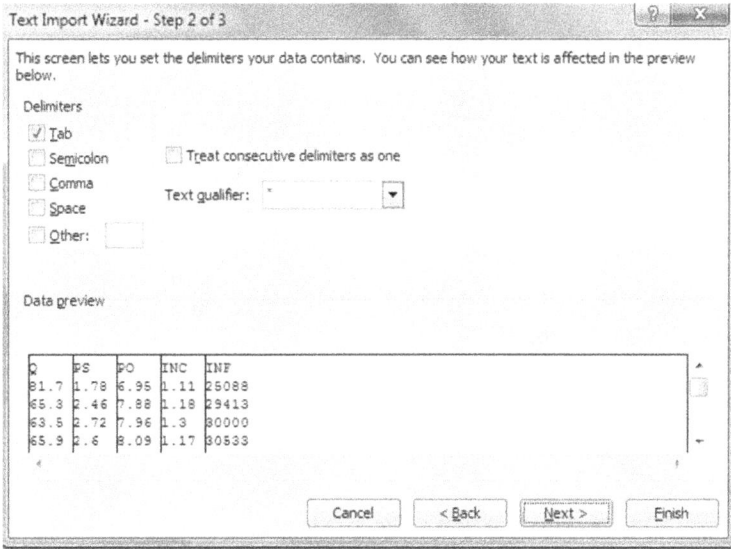

Figure 1.5 Second text wizard dialog box

Once we have the data in Excel, we can change any cell format by first right-clicking the cell and then clicking Format Cells, which opens the Format Cells dialog box where we will find many tools for changing the cells, or we can refer to Vu (2015) for more instructions.

Deleting Every X Rows

Touro asks,

> I have monthly sales data for my Touristo company. My boss wants me to compare it with data from other companies. However, they only have data for January, April, July, and October. Can you teach us how to delete every two months from my data without Excel programing?.

> Invo says that he knows how to do it and tells Touro to show us the data in the file Ch01. Fig.1.6. Invo then tells us to perform the following steps:

> Type D into cell C1 (for "delete").
> Type A into cell C2.

Type B into cells C3 and C4.

Highlight cells C2, C3, and C4.

Point at the bottom-right corner of cell C3 to get the Fill Handle, which is a black plus sign (+).

Hold down your left mouse clicker and drag this Fill Handle to the end of the dataset.

Copy data in columns A, B, and C, then paste it into columns E, F, and G so that you can keep the original data.

Highlight columns E, F, and G.

Go to Data on the ribbon, then click Sort.

A dialog box appears.

In the Sort by box, choose D and click OK.

Now you will see all As from cells G2 through G13.

Cells E2 through F13 in the data file show data for January, April, July, and October.

Tourp tells us to delete the irrelevant data and transpose cells E2 through F13 into the horizontal format if we wish to display the results as shown in Figure 1.6.

Professor Empirie says that for deleting columns, use the Paste Special tools discussed in the previous section to transpose the columns to rows so that you can sort the data in rows. Once the unwanted data are deleted, transpose the data back to columns.

Calculating in Excel

The following commands are needed to obtain calculation results in Excel.

For adding variable X in cell A2 to variable Y in cell B2: Type =$A2+B2$ into any empty cell, then press Enter.

For multiplying (or dividing) X in cell A2 by Y in cell B2: Type =$A2*B2$ in an empty cell (or $A2/B2$), then press Enter.

	H	I	J	K	L	M	N	O	P	Q	R	S	T	U
1	Month	January	April	July	October	January	April	July	October	January	April	July	October
2	Sale	71.71	54.96	71.92	67.60	49.77	69.44	84.48	86.96	104.16	63.45	86.79	57.45

Fig 1.1 Fig 1.2 Fig 1.5 Table 1.3

Figure 1.6 Deleting unwanted data

For obtaining X^b in cell A2: Type *=A2^(b)* in an empty cell, then press Enter.

For the logarithm in cell A2: Type *=ln(A2)* in an empty cell, then press Enter.

For the sum X = $(X_1 + X_2 + X_3)$ with X_1, X_2, and X_3 in cells A1, A2, A3, respectively:

Type *=SUM(A1:A3)* in an empty cell, then press Enter.

For the average (or standard deviation) of the same X: Replace the word SUM in the preceding formula with AVERAGE (or STDEV).

Taila asks,

I have data on expenditure on inputs for 200 weeks from my Tailorie shop. I wish to organize this data into five-week intervals so that I can know how much of each input to order from a supply chain every five weeks. Can you teach us how to calculate the above three statistics for equal intervals of five weeks?

Professor Empirie says yes and asks Taila to show us the data for the first 10 weeks for demonstration purpose. Taila tells us to open the file *Ch01.xls. Table 1.4.* We see that she lists three types of inputs for her shop—namely, buttons, zippers, and threads. We need to perform the following steps:

First, copy data in cells B1 through D1 and paste into cells F1 through H1.

(This gives us the labels of the three variables.)

In cell F2 type *=SUM(B2:B6)*, then press Enter.

Copy the formula in cell F2 and paste into cells G2 and H2.

Highlight the block of cells F2 through H6.

Copy this block of cells F2 through H6 and paste into cells F7 through H11.

For the averages (or standard deviations), replace the word SUM in the preceding formula with AVERAGE (or STDEV) and change the cells accordingly.

Table 1.4 Basic descriptive statistics of input demand for Tailorie

Statistics	Sum		Mean		Standard deviation	
Week	1 to 5	6 to 10	11 to 15	1 to 5	6 to 10	11 to 15
Button	8.12	6.58	1.62	1.32	0.30	0.09
Zipper	39.12	42.41	7.82	8.48	0.51	0.32
Thread	5.71	6.36	1.14	1.27	0.13	0.17

Professor Empirie says that this trick will save a lot of time if you have hundreds of data points as Taila does. Once we finish calculating all three statistics, we need to eliminate the formulas using the Paste Special tools and click Values. We can also use the commands for deleting every X rows to eliminate the blank cells and the Paste Special tools to transpose the data. The final results are shown in Table 1.4.

To conclude the chapter, Professor Empirie says that we can also use the mathematical functions to obtain the sum, average, standard deviation, and so on by clicking on the letter f_x, which is located below and to the left of the word "Alignment" on the ribbon. For example, click f_x and choose SUM and then click OK. A dialog box appears. Type in B2:B6, then click OK. This yields the sum of the values in cells B2 through B6.

Exercises

1. Let X be a discrete random variable with the values $X = 0, 3, 2$ and the probabilities

$$P(X = 0) = 0.30,$$
$$P(X = 3) = 0.40,$$
$$P(X = 2) = 0.30,$$

(a) Calculate $E(X)$
(b) Find $Var(X)$
(c) Given a new function

$$g(X) = 4X + 3,$$

find the expectation and variance of this function.

2. Data on demand for travels are provided by Touro in the file Travels in the folder Data for Exercise. Draw a histogram using Excel and put the data into a table similar to Table 1.2 in this chapter.

3. Data on sale values provided by Invo are in the file Portfolios.xls in the folder Data for Exercise. Calculate the sum, mean, and standard deviation of the series using Excel mathematic operations.

CHAPTER 2

Simple Linear Regression

Touro currently works part-time for the travel agency Tourista. His boss wanted him to estimate how demand for nondurable goods and services, from the population in general and from tourists in particular, would be affected by an increase in minimum wage in the state. Thus, he can't wait to start this chapter, knowing that once he finishes with it, he will be able to:

1. Develop econometric models for simple linear regression;
2. Distinguish between the regression estimators and the estimates;
3. Analyze basic concepts for t-tests and goodness-of-fit measurements;
4. Perform data analyses and interpret the results using Excel.

Econometric Models

Prof. Metric reminds us that an econometric model is used to estimate the possible effect of an explanatory variable on a dependent variable. Chapter 1 has the following econometric model:

$$SPEND = a_1 + a_2\ WAGE + e, \qquad (2.1)$$

where SPEND is the spending on nondurable goods and services of a representative consumer, and WAGE his or her average weekly wage. The parameter a_1 is the intercept and a_2 the slope of the regression line. The random error e accounts for a set of unobserved factors (other than WAGE or any random component in the model) that might affect SPEND.

A general model for any variables is written as:

$$y = a_1 + a_2\ x + e. \qquad (2.2)$$

Since e captures the random component of y, we have the following equation for the regression line:

$$E(y|x) = a_1 + a_2 x. \tag{2.3}$$

Booka raises her hand and asks, "Can anyone explain the notation $E(y|x)$?" Invo offers an explanation as follows:

> $E(y|x)$ is called the expectation of y given x. In Chapter 1, we learned to find $E(X)$, which is expectation of X given several values of X such as $x_1, x_2, \ldots, x_n$. In this chapter, I think we are learning a new concept $E(y|x)$, which implies that expectation of y is dependent on x instead of on several values of itself such as $y_1, y_2, \ldots,$ y_n. For this reason, I believe that $E(y|x)$, which is also written as $E(y|x = x_i)$, is classified as a conditional expectation and the whole function is called the conditional expectation function.

Prof. Metric commends Invo on his correct observation and points out that the error term e is the difference between actual y and its mean, as deduced from equations (2.2) and (2.3):

$$e = y - E(y|x) = y - (a_1 + a_2 x).$$

This error term also captures any estimation error that arises and any random behavior that might present in each individual identity.

Prof. Metric says that we will consider two types of data in this section: cross sectional and time series. A cross-sectional dataset presents many identities, which can be individuals, cities, states, and so on, in a single period. A time-series dataset tracks a single identity over many periods, which can be days, weeks, months, years, and so forth. Regarding cross-sectional data, the subscript i refers to the entity being observed, and the six classic assumptions are:

(i) The model is given by a linear function

$$y_i = a_1 + a_2 x_i + e_i.$$

(ii) $E(e_i) = E(y_i) = 0$.

(iii) $Var(e_i) = Var(y_i) = \sigma^2$.

(iv) $Cov(e_i, e_j) = Cov(y_i, y_j) = 0$ for $i \neq j$.

 (v) x_i is not random and must take at least two different values.

(vi) $e_i \sim N(0, \sigma^2)$; $y_i \sim ([a_1 + a_2 x_i], \sigma^2)$.

For time-series data, assumption (*v*) changes to:

 (v) y_t and x_t are stationary random variables and must take at least two different values, and e_t is independent of current, past, and future values of x_t.

The remaining assumptions for cross-sectional data hold for time-series data, except that in this textbook the subscript i is changed to t and the subscript j is changed to z.

Regarding the stationarity in assumption (*v*) for time-series data, Prof. Metric says that we can roughly think of a stationary series as one that is neither explosive nor wandering aimlessly and that we will discuss this concept in detail in the later chapters. We also learn that data with the constant variance for all samples are said to be *homoskedastic*, and data with different variances for different samples are said to be *heteroscedastic*, which will be discussed in Chapter 4.

Simple linear regression often uses the least squares technique, also called ordinary least squares (OLS), because this technique minimizes the sum of the squared differences between the observed values of y and their expected values $E(y|x)$. If assumptions (*i*) through (*v*) hold, then the Gauss-Markov theorem states that the OLS estimator will produce the best linear unbiased estimators (BLUE). If assumption (*vi*) also holds true, in addition to the other five assumptions, then the test results are valid.

The Central Limit Theorem (CLT) is very convenient for the assumption (*vi*). The theorem states that given a sufficiently large sample size from a population with a finite level of variance, the mean of all samples from the same population will be close to the mean of the population. In addition, all variances will be close to the variance of the population divided by each sample's size. In this case, the test results are valid.

Taila then asks, "What do they mean by *sufficiently large*?" Prof. Metric commends her on the question and says that the question of "how large is large enough" is a matter of interpretation, but a cross-sectional sample with 30 data points or a time-series sample with 20 data points is usually considered large enough to cite CLT for valid test results.

Estimators and Estimates

Interpreting Coefficient Estimates

We learn that we need to collect data for estimations and that the estimated version of equation (2.2) is:

$$\hat{y}_i = \hat{a}_1 + \hat{a}_2 x_i$$
$$y_i = \hat{y}_i + \hat{e}_i = \hat{a}_1 + \hat{a}_2 x_i + \hat{e}_i. \tag{2.4}$$

Prof. Metric says that the derivation of the OLS estimators in a simple linear regression needs knowledge of calculus and can be found in Verbeek (2012). We are only required to know that the estimators for the parameters $\hat{a}_1$ and $\hat{a}_2$ are written as:

$$\hat{a}_2 = \frac{\sum (x_i - \bar{x})(y_i - \bar{y})}{\sum (x_i - \bar{x})^2} \text{ and } \hat{a}_1 = \bar{y} - \hat{a}_2 \bar{x}, \tag{2.5}$$

where $\bar{x}$ is the sample mean of x, and $\bar{y}$ is that of y.

Specific values for $\hat{a}_1$ and $\hat{a}_2$ are called coefficient estimates (or estimates for short). Some econometricians also call them estimated coefficients. They are in fact point estimates, which provide a single value for each parameter of the OLS regression.

Once each parameter is estimated, the OLS estimates are interpreted according to the econometric model we develop. In general, the intercept $\hat{a}_1$ estimates the parameter a_1, which measures the number of unit changes in y when x is zero, whereas the slope $\hat{a}_2$ estimates a_2, which measures the number of unit changes in y due to a unit change in x.

$$a_2 = \frac{\Delta y}{\Delta x} \text{ for a theoretical model, or}$$

$$a_2 = \frac{\Delta E(y)}{\Delta x} \text{ for an econometric model} \tag{2.6}$$

For example, the intercept in equation (2.1) represents a person's spending on nondurable goods when his or her wage is zero, whereas the slope represents the number of unit changes in spending due to a unit change in weekly wage. If wage is the only source of income for this representative consumer, then the slope measures the marginal propensity in nondurable spending.

The slope of an OLS regression can be used to measure elasticity as well. Theoretically, the equation for elasticity is:

$$\varepsilon = \frac{\%\Delta y}{\%\Delta x} = \frac{\Delta y / y}{\Delta x / x} = \frac{\Delta y}{\Delta x} \cdot \frac{x}{y}$$

In econometrics, we can use the expressions in equation (2.6) to write the formula for calculating elasticity:

$$\varepsilon = \frac{\Delta E(y) / E(y)}{\Delta x / x} = \frac{\Delta E(y)}{\Delta x} \cdot \frac{x}{E(y)} = a_2 \frac{x}{E(y)}$$

Hence, the estimation of elasticity is:

$$\varepsilon = a_2 \frac{x}{E(y)} \text{ theoretically and } \varepsilon = \hat{a}_2 \frac{\bar{x}}{\bar{y}} \text{ empirically,} \qquad (2.7)$$

where the definitions of the variables are the same as those in the previous sections.

Prof. Metric says that there is a special case when both sides of equation (2.2) are in natural logarithmic form so that we have data for percentage change of y and percentage change of x. In this case, we do not have to follow equation (2.7), because $\hat{a}_2$ itself will measure percentage change of y due to one percent change of x, which is the elasticity.

Point Estimates

We learn that equation (2.5) can be used to calculate the point estimates of the OLS regression. Since all econometric software provide point estimates, Prof. Metric refers us to Table 2.1 at the end of the chapter, so that we can follow the steps provided in this table to practice calculating those point estimates of $\hat{a}_1$ and $\hat{a}_2$.

Suppose that substituting all variables into equation (2.5) yields $\hat{a}_2 = 0.5$ and $\hat{a}_1 = 1.5$, then the equation for the regression line becomes:

$$\hat{y}_i = 1.5 + 0.5\, x_i,$$

where 1.5 is the intercept and 0.5 is the slope of the line.

Invo exclaims, "Oh, if we let y be weekly spending and x weekly wage, both in hundreds of dollars, then the results imply that

(i) Weekly spending of a person without wage is $150 (= 1.5*$100), and

(ii) A $100 increase in weekly wage raises spending by $50 (= 0.5*$100)."

Prof. Metic commends Invo for his correct answers and moves to the next topic.

Interval Estimates

Prof. Metric says that in the previous subsection we only learned how to calculate point estimates. These point estimates do not account for any uncertainty in everyday life. Hence, we need to learn how to calculate an interval estimate, which provides a range of values instead of one single value for each parameter. This will allow us to face any uncertainty and still be able to state with a certain level of confidence that the actual value will likely fall between the upper and lower bounds (also called the end-points) of this range.

To calculate interval estimates, a t-distribution for a sample of N observations is given as:

$$t = \frac{\hat{a}_k - a_k}{se\left(\hat{a}_k\right)} \sim t_{(N-2)} \text{ for } k = 1 \text{ or } 2 \text{ in simple regression,} \qquad (2.8)$$

where $N-2$ = the degrees of freedom (df) for the simple linear regression,

a_k = the parameters to be estimated,

$\hat{a}_k$ = the coefficient estimate from the OLS regression, and

$se(\hat{a}_k)$ = the standard error of the coefficient estimate.

We learned earlier that if the classic assumptions (*i*) through (*vi*) hold, then the OLS estimators a_1 and a_2 have normal distribution. The same is true for $\hat{a}_1$ and $\hat{a}_2$.

$$\hat{a}_2 \sim N\left(a_2, \text{var}(\hat{a}_2)\right),$$

where $\text{var}(a_2) = \sigma^2 / \sum(x_i - \bar{x})^2$.

Prof. Metric reminds us of a statistics concept, in which a standardized normal random variable Z is obtained as follows:

$$Z = \frac{\hat{a}_2 - a_2}{\sqrt{\text{var}(\hat{a}_2)}} \sim N(0,1).$$

A similar formula can be written for a_1. Given a critical value of $Z(Z_c)$—for instance, α is the probability that the value is in the tail of the distribution—then the interval estimator is:

$$P\left[\hat{a}_k - Z_c * se\left(\hat{a}_k\right) \le a_k \le \hat{a}_k + Z_c * se\left(\hat{a}_k\right)\right] = 1 - \alpha.$$

The CLT allows us to use the estimated values for the *t*-distribution as a substitution for Z when a sample is large enough. In that case, a *t*-critical value from the *t*-distribution is given so that

$$P\left[\hat{a}_k - t_c * se\left(\hat{a}_k\right) \le a_k \le \hat{a}_k + t_c * se\left(\hat{a}_k\right)\right] = 1 - \alpha. \quad (2.9)$$

Equation (2.9) provides an interval estimator of a_k. The interval is expressed as a $100(1 - \alpha)\%$ confidence interval. For example, if we choose $\alpha = 0.01$, then the confidence interval is 99 percent—that is, we are 99 percent confident that the actual value falls somewhere between the lower bound and the upper bound of the interval estimate.

Prof. Metric says that we can choose a 90 percent confidence interval ($\alpha = 0.10$) or a 95 percent confidence interval ($\alpha = 0.05$) or a 99 percent confidence interval ($\alpha = 0.01$). Most of the time, we choose the middle value ($\alpha = 0.05$). Note that the interval has an upper bound and a lower bound. Hence, we will have to divide α into two tails, $\alpha/2 = 0.025$, so that the total value of α is 0.05 ($\alpha = 0.025 + 0.025 = 0.05$) and the confidence interval is 95 percent.

He then gives us an example: Suppose the sample size is N = 32 (df = 30), $\hat{a}_2$ = 0.5, and se ($\hat{a}_2$) = 0.1. Choosing a 95 percent confidence interval so that α = 0.05, we calculate the interval as follows.

On each of the two tails, $\alpha/2$ = 0.025. We then look at a t-table for a critical value and find that $t_C = t_{(0.975, 30)}$ = 2.042. Taila tells us that we can also type = $TINV(0.05, 30)$ into any Excel cell to obtain $t_C = t_{(0.975, 30)}$ = 2.042. We are very impressed with her intelligence. We find that the interval estimate for a_2 is:

$$0.5 \pm 2.042*0.1 = 0.5 \pm 0.2042 = (0.2958; 0.7042).$$

Touro exclaims, "Oh, then we are 95% confident that a $100 increase in weekly wage will raise nondurable spending anywhere from $29.58 to $70.42, depending on, I guess, the individual characteristics." Prof. Metric praises Touro for the correct interpretation and guides us to the next topic.

Estimating Var(e_i)

Invo recalls equation (1.6) for variance and volunteers to write:

$$Var\left(e_i\right) = \sigma^2 = E\left[e_i - E\left(e_i\right)\right]^2 = E\left(e_i^2\right). \qquad (2.10)$$

We are wondering why the second term in the formula disappears. Invo explains, "Assumption (ii) tells us that $E(e_i) = E(y_i) = 0$." We now realize that what he says is true and guess that we can take the average of the squared errors as an estimator of σ^2, which is written as:

$$Estimated\ \sigma^2 = s^2 = Estimated\ E\left(e_i^2\right) = \frac{\sum e_i^2}{N}.$$

It turns out that this formula does not help, because the errors e_i are unknown. Prof. Metric tells us to recall the error term in equation (2.3) and the analog of it—namely, the OLS residual in equation (2.4). We are able to derive the following expressions from these two equations:

$$e_i = y_i - \left(a_1 + a_2 x_i\right),$$
$$\hat{e}_i = y_i - \left(\hat{a}_1 + \hat{a}_2 x_i\right).$$

Since their error terms are similar, we guess that we can use the regression residual $\hat{e}_i$ in place of the errors e_i:

$$Estimated\ \sigma^2 = s^2 = Estimated\ E\left(\hat{e}_i^2\right) = \frac{\sum \hat{e}_i^2}{N}.$$

Touro says that this formula seems to have the same problem as the one in equation (1.7). Prof. Metric says that Touro is correct and refers us to equation (1.8) so that we can write an unbiased estimator of σ^2 as:

$$Estimated\ \sigma^2 = s^2 = Estimated\ E\left(\hat{e}_i^2\right) = \frac{\sum \hat{e}_i^2}{N-2}. \qquad (2.11)$$

Taila exclaims, "Wow, we must have learned to estimate all parameters in this simple linear regression model." Prof. Metric smiles and says, "No, we have one more parameter to estimate: the predicted value of y, and equation (2.11) will be helpful for the interval prediction of y."

Predicted Value

We learn that once coefficient estimates are obtained, the value of y, called the predicted value, can be calculated by substituting these parameters into the model. From Table 2.1, the prediction for y when $x = 6$ (that is, $600) can be calculated using equation (2.4) as follows:

$$\hat{y} = 1.5 + 0.5*6 = 1.5 + 3 = 4.5\ (\$\ hundreds) = \$450.$$

Thus, a person with a weekly wage of $600 will spend $450 on non-durable goods and services.

Prof. Metric says that interval prediction can also be calculated in a similar manner using the standard error of the prediction $se(p)$ for the model. Let $\hat{y}_1 = \hat{a}_1 + \hat{a}_2 x_1$, then a formula in Kmenta (1997) can be used for calculating an approximation of the $se(p)$:

$$se\left(p\right) = s\sqrt{1 + \frac{1}{N} + \frac{\left(x_1 - \bar{x}\right)^2}{\sum\left(x_i - \bar{x}\right)^2}};\quad s = \sqrt{\frac{\sum \hat{e}_i^2}{N-2}} = \sqrt{\frac{SSE}{N-2}} \qquad (2.12)$$

where s = the standard error of the regression, which is the square root of s^2 in equation (2.11) and

SSE = the sum of the squared errors, which are often called the residuals in regression.

The interval prediction is calculated by replacing $se(\hat{a}_k)$ in equation (2.9) with $se(p)$:

$$P\left[\hat{y}_1 - t_c se\left(\mathrm{p}\right) \leq y_1 \leq \hat{y}_1 + t_c se\left(\mathrm{p}\right)\right] = 1 - a. \qquad (2.13)$$

Prof. Metric then tells us to use the aforementioned point estimate of $450 for weekly spending and calculate an interval prediction. He gives us $se(p)$ = 0.5, N = 32, and α = 0.05. We are able to look at a t-table for a critical value and find that $t_C = t_{(0.975,\ 30)}$ = 2.042, so the two endpoints of the interval prediction for weekly spending are:

$$4.5 \pm 2.042*0.5 = (3.479;\ 5.521).$$

Hence, we predict with 95 percent confidence that a person with a weekly wage of $600 will spend anywhere from $347.90 (the lower bound) to $552.10 (the upper bound) every week.

Hypothesis Testing

Prof. Metric says that t-tests are used to verify the statistical significance or the expected values of the regression coefficients. Since simple linear regression has only one independent variable, the t-test for the significance of $\hat{a}_2$ also serves as the test for model significance.

Four Standard Steps

A t-test is usually carried out in four standard steps, shown as follows:

(i) State the hypotheses.
   Define a constant c as a specific value for a parameter that we want to test.

If the null H_o is $a_k \leq c$, then the alternative H_a is $a_k > c$.

If the null H_o is $a_k \geq c$, then the alternative H_a is $a_k < c$.

If the null H_o is $a_k = c$, then the alternative H_a could be $a_k > c$ or $a_k < c$ or $a_k \neq c$.

(ii) The test statistic:

$$t_{STAT} = t = \frac{\hat{a}_k - c}{se\left(\hat{a}_k\right)} \sim t_{(N-2)},$$

where $k = 1$ or 2 in a simple regression. (2.14)

(iii) The critical t-value, t_C, which indicated the border point of the rejection region, depends on the significance level of the test, which is usually at 1%, 3%, or 10%.

(iv) Decision: If $|t_{STAT}| \geq t_C$, we reject the null and follow the alternative hypothesis. Otherwise, we do not reject the null. We then draw the meaning and the implication of our decision concerning the parameters of a regression.

We learn that there are two basic types of t-tests: If c is any constant other than zero, we have a test of a general hypothesis; and if c is zero, we have a test of significance, because a parameter only has a significant impact on a model if it is not zero. Prof. Metric emphasizes to us that the tails of the tests always follow the alternative hypotheses. There are only three cases: in the alternative hypothesis (H_a), if $a_k > c$, we have a right-tailed test; if $a_k < c$, we have a left-tailed test; and if $a_k \neq c$, we have a two-tailed test.

Tests of the General Hypothesis

Booka offers an example. Last week she wanted to find out the demand for books in relation to income. The dependent variable is spending on books (BOOK), and the independent variable is per capita income (PERCA). She found the following relationship between the two variables: BOOK = 0.09*PERCA, and $se(\hat{a}_2) = 0.015$. Booka says that she conducted a survey of 34 customers, so $N = 34$. We proceed to perform several tests as follows:

A right-tailed test

Invo says, "Let's test the alternative hypothesis $a_2 > 0.06$ against the null hypothesis $a_2 \leq 0.06$." We agree with him and perform the test as follows:

(i) $H_0: a_2 \leq 0.06$; $H_a: a_2 > 0.06$.

(ii) $t_{STAT} = t_{(N-2)} = (0.09 - 0.06)/0.015 = 2$.

(iii) We decide to choose $\alpha = 0.05$, so $t_C = t_{(0.95, 32)} = 1.694$.

Prof. Metric says that Excel always reports a two-tailed critical value, so to find t-critical for a one-tailed test, type $= TINV(2\alpha, df)$ into any cell, then press Enter.

For example, typing $= TINV(0.10, 32)$ into any empty cell and then pressing the Enter key yields the result of $1.6939 \approx 1.694$.

(iv) Decision: Since $|t_{STAT}| > t_C$, we reject the null (H_0), meaning $a_2 > 0.06$, thus implying that the customers of the bookshop tend to spend more than 6 percent of the increase in their income on books.

A left-tailed test

Touro wants us to test the alternative hypothesis $a_2 < 0.15$ against the null hypothesis $a_2 \geq 0.15$. We proceed with the test as follows:

(i) $H_0: a_2 \geq 0.15$; $H_a: a_2 < 0.15$.

(ii) $t_{STAT} = t_{(N-2)} = (0.09 - 0.15)/0.015 = -4$.

(iii) We try $\alpha = 0.01$ this time, so $t_C = t_{(99, 32)} = 2.449$ (or $(-t_C) = -2.449$). We also type $= TINV(0.02, 32)$ into Excel, which gives us $2.44868 \approx 2.449$.

(iv) Decision: Since $|t_{STAT}| > t_C$ (or $t_{STAT} < (-t_C)$), we reject the null (H_0), meaning $a_2 < 0.15$ and implying that the customers tend to spend less than 15 percent of the increase in their income on books.

Tests of Significance

A one-tailed test

Prof. Metric wants us to test the significance of the slope, so the null hypothesis states that the slope is zero. Since the right-tailed test and the left-tailed test are very similar, we choose to test the alternative hypothesis for $a_2 > 0$:

(i) $H_0: a_2 = 0$; $H_a: a_2 > 0$.

(ii) $t_{STAT} = t_{(N-2)} = (0.09 - 0)/0.015 = 0.09/0.015 = 6$.

(iii) We decide to choose $\alpha = 0.01$ again, so $t_C = t_{(0.99, \, 32)} = 2.449$.

(iv) Decision: Since $|t_{(N-2)}| > t_C = t_{(0.99, \, 32)}$, we reject the null, meaning $a_2 > 0$ and implying that income has a positive effect on book spending.

A two-tailed test

This time, Booka wants to test the alternative $a_2 \neq 0$. Prof. Metric agrees and says that the left-tailed test of significance is similar to the right-tailed test, so we do not have to try it in the class. We now perform the two-tailed test as follows.

(i) $H_0: a_2 = 0; \ H_1: a_2 \neq 0$.

(ii) $t_{STAT} = t_{(N-2)} = (0.09 - 0)/0.015 = 0.09/0.015 = 6$.

(iii) Since this is a two-tailed test, Prof. Metric reminds us to use $\alpha/2 = 0.025$, and so

$$t_C = t_{(0.975, \, 32)} = 2.037.$$

For a two-tailed test, we learn to type $=TINV(\alpha, \, df)$ into any cell in Excel.

So, we type $=TINV(0.05, \, 32)$, then press Enter. Excel gives us $2.0369 \approx 2.037$.

(iv) Decision: Since $|t_{STAT}| > t_C$, we again reject the null, meaning $a_2 \neq 0$ and implying that income does have a significant impact on book spending. We also recall the earlier discussion and are able to state that the model is statistically significant as well.

Prof. Metric reminds us that Excel reports the t_{STAT} value for the two-tailed test of significance—that is, in the null hypothesis (H_0) $a_k = 0$ and in the alternative hypothesis (H_a) $a_k \neq 0$. This t_{STAT} is also called the t-ratio because we only need to divide a_k by $se(a_k)$ when $c = 0$. You will hear about this t-ratio from a lot of researchers because it is one of the most important statistics in econometric study.

Goodness-of-Fit and P-Value

Taila asks, "How can I compare two models and find out exactly which one predicts better?" Prof. Metric says enthusiastically that it is quite possible to do this, and that it is called "goodness-of-fit." We will learn about goodness-of-fit in this section.

R-squared (R²)

We learn that an R^2 value can measure how much the variation in y can be explained by the variation in x. In the first section, we have the estimated equation as:

$$y_i = \hat{y}_i + \hat{e}_i.$$

Subtracting the sample mean from both sides of this equation gives us:

$$y_i - \bar{y} = \left(\hat{y}_i - \bar{y}\right) + \hat{e}_i.$$

Square both sides of the previous equation and take the sum of these expressions to obtain:

$$\sum\left(y_i - \bar{y}\right)^2 = \sum\left(\hat{y}_i - \bar{y}\right)^2 + 2\sum\left(\hat{y}_i - \bar{y}\right)\hat{e}_i + \sum\hat{e}_i^2.$$

We know that the cross term $2\sum(\hat{y}_i - \bar{y})\hat{e}_i$ is zero because E $(\hat{e}) = 0$, so

$$\sum\left(y_i - \bar{y}\right)^2 = \sum\left(\hat{y}_i - \bar{y}\right)^2 + \sum\hat{e}_i^2. \qquad (2.15)$$

The following definitions are commonly used for the squared terms in equation (2.15).

$\sum(y_i - \bar{y})^2$ = the total sum of squares (SST)
$\sum(\hat{y}_i - \bar{y})^2$ = the sum of squares of the regression (SSR)
$\sum\hat{e}_i^2$ = the sum of squared errors (SSE).

Given these definitions, the R^2 value is the coefficient of determination and is defined as

$$R^2 = \frac{SSR}{SST} = 1 - \frac{SSE}{SST}. \qquad (2.16)$$

If $R^2 = 1$, the model is said to have a perfect fit. In practice, we always find that $0 < R^2 < 1$. R^2 is reported by all econometric packages, including Excel. If R^2 is high, then the model is a good fit; for example, $R^2 = 0.92$ implies that 92 percent of the variation in the dependent variable can be explained by the independent variable. If R^2 is low, then the model is not a good fit.

Prof. Metric points out that in Figure 2.2 of the Data Analyses section, SSR, SSE, and SST are reported in cells H12, H13, and H14, respectively.

P-Value

We learn that *p*-values can be used to measure the exact significance level of the aforementioned estimates. A p-value indicates the probability that a random variable falls into the rejection region at a particular significance level. Invo exclaims, "Sounds too abstract for me to understand. Can anyone explain more clearly what p-values really measure?"

Taila offers an explanation,

> When we run a regression, the null hypothesis is the possibility that there is no effect on our results. For example, an experiment for a medical treatment that we know is totally ineffective. The null hypothesis is true: there is no difference between the experimental groups at the population level. Despite the null being true, it is possible that there will be an effect in the sample data due to random sampling error. P-values measure how well the sample data support the argument that this medical treatment has no effect. A high p-value implies our data are likely with a true null, and a low p-value implies our data are not likely with a true null. In the above example, a low p-value suggests that your sample provides enough evidence for you to reject the null of no effect in the medical treatment.

Prof. Metric praises Taila and provides us a numerical example: A p-value = 0.002 for a model implies that we reject the null at a 0.2 percent significance level, which is a very good fit because we need the model to satisfy only 5 percent significance level. A formula for calculating p-values is introduced in Hill et al. (2011), but most econometric packages, including Excel, report p-values, so we do not have to learn this skill.

Thanks to this practice, we can look up p-values instead of going through the steps of calculating t_{STAT} and depending on the t-table for t-critical values. We can always reject the null hypothesis if the p-value $\leq \alpha$, where α could be 0.01, 0.05, or 0.10. For example, if we choose $\alpha = 0.05$, then we reject the null if the p-value ≤ 0.05. The following values are generally used for the tests of coefficient significances:

If p-value ≤ 0.01: the coefficient estimate is highly significant.
If $0.01 <$ p-value ≤ 0.05: the coefficient estimate is significant.
If $0.05 <$ p-value ≤ 0.10: the coefficient estimate is weakly significant.
If p-value > 0.10: the coefficient estimate is not statistically significant.

Prof. Metric asks us to look at Figure 2.2 in the Data Analyses section in order to practice how to interpret p-values: From this figure, the coefficient estimate of the intercept is reported in cell J17 and it is only weakly significant (with p-value = 0.065); whereas, the slope estimate is reported in cell J18 and it is highly significant (with p-value = $1.398*10^{-29}$). Invo exclaims, "I see another value of $1.398*10^{-29}$ reported in cell K12. Is that the p-value for the significance of the whole model?" Prof. Metric commends him on the remark and says that this is true.

Data Analyses

Performing a Regression

Prof. Empirie says that we usually have three types of data for performing regression: cross sectional, time series, and longitudinal/panel. We discussed cross-sectional and time-series data at the beginning of this chapter. A longitudinal/panel dataset follows many identities over many periods.

Prof. Empirie reminds us again that all data are available in the folder Data Analyses.

Invo has collected data on expenditure on durables (DUR) and personal income (INCOME) for 51 cities (ID) in 2015. He tells us that the dataset is too large to display but is available in the file *Ch02.xls. Fig.2.1-2.2.* We want to see if DUR depends on INCOME—that is, if DUR is the dependent variable and INCOME the independent variable. We open the data file and follow these steps to perform a regression of DUR on INCOME:

Select Data and then Data Analysis on the ribbon.

Click Regression in the list instead of Descriptive Statistics, then click OK.

A dialog box appears, as shown in Figure 2.1.

Type B1:B52 into the Input Y Range box.

Type C1:C52 into the Input X Range box.

Select the Labels and Residuals boxes.

Select the Output Range button and enter F1.

Click OK; you will see another dialog box stating that data will be overridden.

Click OK again to overwrite the data.

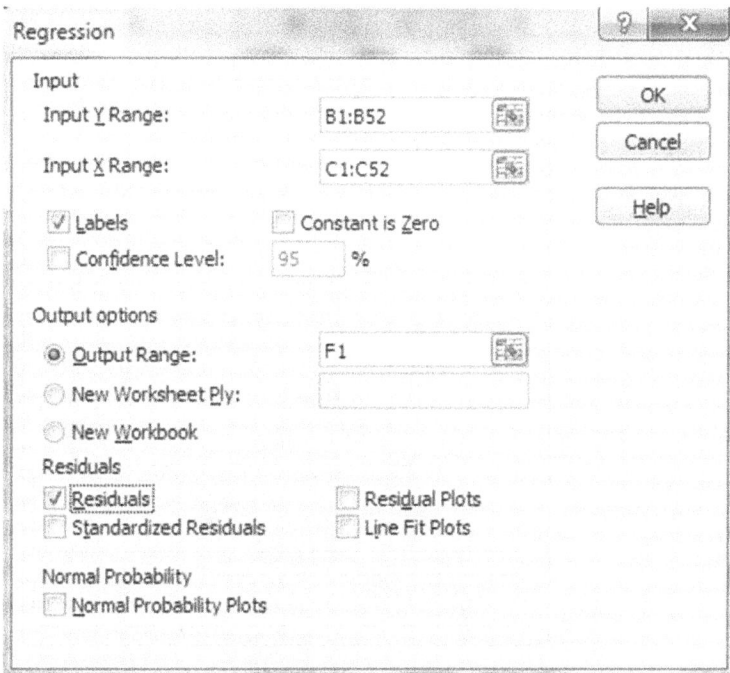

Figure 2.1 Performing regression: Commands in dialog box

	E	F	G	H	I	J	K	L	M	N
1		SUMMARY OUTPUT								
2										
3		*Regression Statistics*								
4		Multiple R	0.963078632							
5		R Square	0.927520451							
6		Adjusted R Square	0.926041276							
7		Standard Error	9929.877105							
8		Observations	51							
9										
10		ANOVA								
11			*df*	*SS*	*MS*	*F*	*Significance F*			
12		Regression	1	61828945224	6.183E+10	627.05277	1.3982E-29			
13		Residual	49	4831520506	98602459					
14		Total	50	66660465730						
15										
16			*Coefficients*	*Standard Error*	*t Stat*	*P-value*	*Lower 95%*	*Upper 95%*	*ower 95.0%*	*pper 95.0%*
17		Intercept	-3453.017678	1829.046726	-1.887878	0.0649713	-7128.62468	222.58933	-7128.62	222.5893
18		INCOME	0.120452156	0.004810193	25.041022	1.398E-29	0.11078571	0.1301186	0.110786	0.130119

Figure 2.2 Simple linear regression results

The regression results are shown in Figure 2.2. Prof. Empirie then guides us to study Figure 2.2 and writes the estimated results (also called estimated equation) as follows:

$$DUR_i = -3453 + 0.1205\ INCOME_i.$$

$$(se) \qquad (1829)\ (0.0048) \qquad R^2 = 0.9275$$

To obtain the predicted value for DUR in 2016, we need to substitute any value of INCOME for a city into this equation. It turns out that when we click Residuals, Excel automatically calculates predicted values and reports them next to the residuals. For example, you can find the predicted DUR for the first city in cell G25 of the data file for Figure 2.2, which is 20,489.25.

Taila points out that she also found the upper and lower 95 percent bounds for the coefficient estimates in cells K17 through L18, which are repeated in cells M17 through N18. Prof. Empirie praises her for her keen observation and says that Excel does not report the interval estimates for the predicted values, so if we wish to know these values, we will have to calculate them using equations (2.7) and (2.8).

She then tells us that we will have opportunities to get hands-on experiences with time-series data and panel data in the later chapters.

Exercises

1. Given the information in Table 2.1, perform the following proce-
   dures:
   (a) Fill in the blank spaces and then use the information in this table
       to calculate $\hat{a}_1$ and $\hat{a}_2$.
   (b) What is the interpretation of $\hat{a}_1$ and $\hat{a}_2$ if the dependent variable
       is yearly salary in ten thousands of dollars and the independent
       variable is college education in years?
2. Given the following estimation results:

$$\text{DEMAND} = 4.198 - 3.229 \text{ PRICE}$$

$$(se)\ (1.012)\ (0.5017) \qquad R^2 = 0.633 \qquad N = 26,$$

   provide comments on the significances of a_1 and the implication of
   the R^2.
3. Use the results in Exercise 2 to test the following hypotheses at a
   1 percent significance level:
   (a) Test the slope is −3 against the alternative hypothesis that the
       slope is smaller than −3.
   (b) Test the slope is zero against the alternative hypothesis that the
       slope is not zero.

   Write the testing procedure in four standard steps similar to
   those in the text. The calculations of the t-statistics may be performed using a handheld calculator or using Excel.

Table 2.1 *Information for calculating coefficient estimates*

Variable	x	$\bar{x}$	y	$\bar{y}$	$(x-\bar{x})^2$	$(x-\bar{x})(y-\bar{y})$
	3		4			
	2		2			
	1		3			
	$\bar{x} =$		$\bar{y} =$		$\sum(x-\bar{x})^2 =$	$\sum(x-\bar{x})(y-\bar{y}) =$

Table 2.2 Information for calculating R^2

y	$\bar{y}$	$y - \bar{y}$	$(y - \bar{y})^2$
2			
−1			
2			
$\bar{y} =$		$\Sigma(y_i - \bar{y}) =$	$\Sigma(y_i - \bar{y})^2 =$

4. Given the information in Table 2.2, fill in the blank spaces and then use the information in this table to calculate R^2 if SSE = 0.60. Provide comments on the result.

5. Data on education expenditures (EDU) and per capita income (PERCA) for 50 states and Washington, DC, in 2014 are in the file Education.xls.

   (a) Perform a regression of PERCA on EDU (dependent variable = y = PERCA; independent variable = x = EDU), write the estimated equation, and find the point predictions for PERCA.

   (b) Provide comments on the coefficient estimates and R^2.

CHAPTER 3

Multiple Linear Regression

Invo tells us that his boss wanted him to examine several factors that can affect consumer spending. Prof. Metric replies that this is one of the topics to be discussed this week and that once we finish the chapter, we will be able to:

1. Develop models for multiple linear regression;
2. Discuss specific issues with the OLS estimation method;
3. Explain basic concepts for *F*-tests and other measurements;
4. Perform data analyses and interpret the results using Excel.

We learn that this chapter will involve two or more explanatory variables.

Econometric Model

So far we have learned to perform regression with only one independent variable. In a real-life situation, we often see more than one factor affecting the movement of a market. Hence, a new model needs to be introduced.

A model with more than one determinant of spending can look like this:

$$SPEND = a_1 + a_2 \, WAGE + a_3 \, HOUSEP, \qquad (3.1)$$

where *SPEND* and *WAGE* are the same as in chapter 2, and *HOUSEP* is the average house price. When house prices go up, consumers feel richer and so increase their spending. The interpretation of a_1 is the same as that in Chapter 2. The interpretation of a_2 and a_3 needs some revision. The parameter a_2 now provides an estimate of the change in consumer spending due to a one-unit change in the wage, *holding HOUSEP constant*.

The parameter a_3 represents the change in consumer spending due to a one-unit change in the average house price, *holding WAGE constant*.

The econometric model derived from equation (3.1) is:

$$SPEND_i = a_1 + a_2\ WAGE_i + a_3\ HOUSEP_i + e_i. \qquad (3.2)$$

For cross-sectional data, the general model is:

$$y_i = a_1 + a_2\ x_{i2} + \ldots + a_k x_{ik} + e_i, \qquad (3.3a)$$

where y is the dependent variable, and the x's are usually called explanatory variables or regressors instead of independent variables because multiple x's might not be completely independent of each other. The interpretation of the slope a_k is:

$$a_k = \frac{\Delta E(y)}{\Delta x_k}\ |\ \text{holding other variables constant.} \qquad (3.3b)$$

Regarding estimations using cross-sectional data, the six classic assumptions in multiple linear regression are:

(i) The model is $y_i = a_1 + a_2\ x_{i2} + \ldots + a_k x_{ik} + e_i$.

(ii) $E(e_i) = E(y_i) = 0$.

(iii) $Var(e_i) = Var(y_i) = \sigma^2$.

(iv) $Cov(e_i, e_j) = Cov(y_i, y_j) = 0$ for $i \neq j$.

(v) Each x_{ik} is not random, must take at least two different values, and is not an exact linear function of any other x.

(vi) $e_i \sim N(0, \sigma^2)$; $y_i \sim ([a_1 + a_2\ x_{i2} + \ldots + a_k x_{ik}], \sigma^2)$.

Assumption (*v*) is modified for time-series data as follows:

(*v.a*) y and x's are stationary random variables, must take at least two different values, and e_t is independent of current, past, and future values of x's.

(*v.b*) when some of the x's are lagged values of y, e_t is uncorrelated to all x's and their past values.

Prof. Metric reminds us,

Assumption (v) only requires that x's are not perfectly correlated to each other. In empirical studies, any correlation of less than 90 percent between two variables can be acceptable; otherwise, they are considered highly correlated with each other, and we will run into the problem of multicollinearity. To overcome this problem, we can replace or eliminate one of the highly correlated variables. We can also modify the model using nonsample information, which will be discussed later in this chapter.

If assumptions (i) through (v) hold, then the OLS technique will produce the BLUE) in multiple linear regression. If assumption (vi) also holds, then test results are valid as long as we can cite the CLT concerning the approximately normal distribution of the errors.

Taila then asks, "What could be the consequences of the multicollinearity problem?" Prof. Metric says that there are several consequences when two or more explanatory variables are highly correlated with each other and continues his explanation. First, the effect of each explanatory variable on the dependent variable Y tends to be imprecise. As indicated in equation (3.1), a regression coefficient approximates the change in the dependent variable due to a one-unit change in an explanatory variable, holding the other variables constant. If variable Z is highly correlated with variable X, a one-unit change in Z causes a change in X, which can no longer be held constant. Second, since the perfectly correlated variables can be written as functions of each other, some of them are redundant. For example, $Z = 2X$, so an estimated equation $Y = a_1 + a_2 Z + a_3 X$ can be written as $Y = a_1 + a_2 2X + a_3 X = a_1 + (2a_2 + a_3) X$. As a result, the estimated equation can be simplified as $Y = a_1 + a_4 X$, and Z is redundant. Third, since some of the explanatory variables are highly correlated with each other, the standard errors of the affected coefficients are often inflated, and the test of the hypothesis that the coefficient is significantly different from zero is less reliable. Finally, because the explanatory variables are highly correlated with each other, small changes to the data of one variable can lead to large changes in the model and might bias the results.

We now see the seriousness of multicollinearity and look forward to learning how to detect and correct the problem.

Estimators and Estimates

We learn that the OLS procedure for multiple linear regression continues to minimize the sum of the squared differences between the observed values of y and their expected values $E(y)$. Let this sum of squares be a function of $a_1, a_2, \ldots, a_k$ then we can write:

$$S\left(a_1, a_2, \ldots \hat{a}_k\right) = S\left(a_1, a_2, \ldots, a_k\right) = \sum_{i=1}^{N}\left[y_i - E\left(y_i\right)\right]^2 =$$

$$\sum_{i=1}^{N}\left[y_i - \left(a_1 + a_2 x_{i2} + \ldots + a_k x_{ik}\right)\right]^2.$$

Prof. Metric says that minimizing this function again can be quite complicated, as one needs knowledge of calculus and the formulas for the estimators are too complicated for us to practice calculating the estimates manually. Hence, the only requirement here is to know that the estimators for multiple regression are $\hat{a}_1, \hat{a}_2, \ldots, \hat{a}_k$, and the estimated equation is:

$$\hat{y}_i = \hat{a}_1 + \hat{a}_2 x_{i2} + \ldots + \hat{a}_k x_{ik}$$
$$y_i = \hat{y}_i + \hat{e}_i = \hat{a}_1 + \hat{a}_2 x_{i2} + \ldots + \hat{a}_k x_{ik} + \hat{e}_i. \tag{3.4}$$

The numeric values of these estimators, which can be obtained from a data analysis of a specific sample using any econometric software, are the estimates of the regression.

Point Estimates

Suppose that estimating equation (3.2) yields the following results:

$$SPEND = 1 + 0.5*WAGE + 0.03 \; HOUSEP, \tag{3.5}$$

where the units are in hundreds of dollars for all three variables, then the results imply that:

(i) Weekly spending of a person without wage is $100.

(ii) Holding the house price constant, $100 increase in weekly wage raises weekly spending by $50.

(iii) Holding the weekly wage constant, $100 increase in the average house price increases weekly spending by $3 (= 0.03*100).

Interval Estimates

Prof. Metric tells us that the equation for interval estimate is the same as in Chapter 2:

$$P\left[\hat{a}_k - t_c * se\left(\hat{a}_k\right) \le a_k \le \hat{a}_k + t_c * se\left(\hat{a}_k\right)\right] = 1 - a. \qquad (3.6)$$

The only difference is that we have K parameters to be estimated in multiple regression. Hence, the t-critical value is based on $(N - K)$ degrees of freedom instead of $(N - 2)$.

Predicted Values

Prof. Metric says that the predicted values can be calculated by substituting the estimated coefficients into the model following a similar procedure discussed in Chapter 2.

In this example, we will substitute the values of wage and house price into equation (3.5) and find that a person with a weekly income of $600 with a change in house price of $1,000 can expect a weekly spending of:

$$SPEND_i = 1 + 0.5*6 + 0.03*10 = 4.3(\$\ hundreds) = \$430. \qquad (3.7)$$

Prof. Metric says that interval predictions can also be made for multiple regression with similar formulas as those in Chapter 2, except for the standard errors:

$$se(\mathrm{p}) = s\sqrt{1 + \frac{1}{N} + \frac{\left(x_1 - \bar{x}\right)^2}{\sum\left(x_i - \bar{x}\right)^2}}; \quad s = \sqrt{\frac{\sum \hat{e}_i^2}{N - K}} = \sqrt{\frac{SSE}{N - K}}. \qquad (3.8)$$

From (3.8), the interval prediction is:

$$P\left[\hat{y}_1 - t_C se(\text{p}) \le y_1 \le \hat{y}_1 + t_C se(\text{p})\right] = 1 - a. \qquad (3.9)$$

In the spending example, if $N = 53$ then $df = 53 - 3 = 50$. We choose $\alpha = 0.05$, so $t_C = 2.009$. Suppose $se(p) = 0.2$, then the interval prediction at a 95 percent confidence interval is:

$$4.3 \pm 2.009*0.2 = (3.8982; 4.7018) = (\$389.82; \$470.18).$$

This result implies that a person with a weekly wage of \$600 will spend anywhere from \$389.82 to \$470.18 weekly when the house price is added to the model and our prediction has a 95 percent confidence interval.

Hypothesis Testing

In order to evaluate each coefficient estimate, a t-test is still appropriate. Prof. Metric says that to determine the joint significance of two or more coefficients or the significance of a model, we need to perform F-tests.

Tests of Joint Significance

Prof. Metric gives us the full model in equation (3.3) with more variables written out here:

$$y_i = a_1 + a_2 x_{i2} + a_3 x_{i3} + a_4 x_{i4} + \ldots + a_k x_{ik} + e_i$$

This model is called an unrestricted model, on which we have to perform a regression and obtain its SSE_U, where U stands for unrestricted. Suppose that we want to test whether a_2 and a_3 are jointly significant, then the restricted model is:

$$y_i = a_1 + a_4 x_{i4} + \ldots + a_k x_{ik} + e_i \qquad (3.10)$$

Hence, we need to perform a regression on this restricted model and obtain its SSE_R, where R stands for restrict. The F-test is then performed in the four standard steps; for equation (3.10) the hypotheses are written as:

(i) H_0: $a_2 = a_3 = 0$; H_a: a_2 and a_3 are jointly significant.

(ii) The F-statistic:

$$F_{STAT} = F = \frac{(SSE_R - SSE_U)/J}{SSE_U/(N-K)} \sim F_{(J,\,N-K)}, \qquad (3.11)$$

where J is called the number of restrictions, which is the number of coefficients in the null hypothesis. The null hypothesis for equation (3.10) only has a_2 and a_3 and so $J = 2$.

(iii) The F-critical value, F_C, can be found from any F-distribution table by choosing α and looking through the table for $F_C = F_{(\alpha,\, J,\, N-K)}$. In Excel, F_C can be found by typing $=FINV(\alpha, J, N - K)$, then pressing Enter.

(iv) Decision: If $F_{STAT} > F_c$, we reject the null hypothesis, meaning the two coefficients are jointly significant and implying that we might not want to eliminate one of them from the regression equation.

Prof. Metric reminds us that an F-distribution has only positive values, so we do not have to compare absolute values of F-statistics to F-critical values. In addition, existing textbooks use various notations for J and $N - K$, as outlined in the following:

J = numerator degrees of freedom = Num. $df = v_2$ (displayed across the top row);

$N - K$ = denominator degrees of freedom = Den. $df = v_1$ (displayed down the column).

He then gives us an unrestricted model with three explanatory variables:

$$SALARY = a_1 + a_2\, EDU + a_3\, EXP + a_4\, IQ + c, \qquad (3.12)$$

where SALARY is the yearly salary and EDU is years of education. EXP is years of experience, IQ (intelligence quotient) score is the same as in section 2, and FED is federal tax credits to residential-property investment. Suppose the regression results for this model are:

SALARY = 0.23 + 0.082 EDU + 0.13 EXP + 0.091 IQ;
(se)   (0.08) (0.02)   (0.05) (0.09)
Number of observations = 51;
SSE_U = 140.

From these results, the coefficient of IQ is insignificant. However, if IQ and EXP are jointly significant, or IQ and EDU are jointly significant, then we might not want to eliminate IQ from the model. To test the joint significance of IQ and EX we need to perform a regression on the restricted model:

$$SALARY = a_1 + a_2 \, EDU + e.$$

Suppose the results for this restricted model are:

SALARY = 0.12 + 0.103 EDU;
(se) (0.07) (0.03)
SSE_R = 170, where R stands for restricted.

We perform the test as follows:

(i) The hypotheses:
   $H_0: a_3 = a_4 = 0$; $H_a: a_3$ and a_4 are jointly significant.
(ii) The F-statistic:
   In this case, $J = 2(a_3$ and $a_4)$, and $(N - K)$ is the degrees of freedom (df). In this case $df = 47 (= 51 - 4)$; hence,

$$F_{STAT} = \frac{(170 - 140)/2}{140/47} = \frac{15}{2.98} = 5.03.$$

(iii) We choose $\alpha = 0.05$, so $F_C = F_{(0.95, 2, 47)} \approx 3.19$.
   In Excel, we can type $=FINV(0.05, 2, 47)$ into any empty cell and then press the Enter key. It gives us the result of 3.195.
(iv) Decision: Since $F_{STAT} > F_C$, we reject the null, meaning the two coefficients are jointly significant and implying that we might not want to eliminate IQ from the regression equation.

Tests of Model Significance

To this point, Booka asks, "What if all coefficients of the explanatory variables in a model are not statistically significant?" Prof. Metric praises her for raising the issue and says that in this case the model does not make any significant contribution to the estimation and should be revised. Thus, we need to test for the model significance, which only needs the full model with its SST and SSE. The four-step procedure for the test is:

(i) H_0: all $a_k = 0$ for $k = 2, 3,..., K$; H_a: at least one $a_k \neq 0$.

(ii) The F-statistic:

$$F_{STAT} = F = \frac{(SST - SSE)/J}{SSE/(N - K)} \sim F_{(J, N-K)},\qquad (3.13)$$

where J is the number of restrictions. Note that in this case, only a_1 is excluded in the null hypothesis because it is for the constant term, so $J = K - 1$.

(iii) F-critical: We learn that we again need to look for $F_C = F_{(\alpha, J, N-K)}$.

(iv) Decision: If $F_{STAT} > F_c$, we reject the null hypothesis. This means at least one $a_k \neq 0$ and implies that the model is statistically significant.

We then work on the example in equation (3.12) with SST given by Prof. Metric as SST = 180. SSE is already given and can be written as SSE = 140 because we have only a single model in (3.12); that is, no subscript U is needed. The four-step procedure for the test is:

(i) H_0: $a_2 = a_3 = a_4 = 0$; H_a: at least one $a_k \neq 0$.

(ii) The F-statistic:

$$F_{STAT} = \frac{(180 - 140)/3}{140/47} = \frac{13.3333}{2.98} = 4.47.$$

Note that $J = K - 1 = 4 - 1 = 3$.

(iii) F-critical: We choose $\alpha = 0.05$, so $F_C = F_{(0.95, 3, 47)} \approx 2.80$.

We also type =FINV(0.05, 3, 47) into an empty cell in Excel and then press Enter. It gives us the same result of 2.8024.

(iv) Decision: If $F_{STAT} > F_c$, we reject the null hypothesis and conclude that at least one $a_k \neq 0$, implying that the model is statistically significant.

F-test Versus t-Test

Tailor suddenly asks, "What are the differences between t-tests and F-tests?" Prof. Metric provides the following explanations.

F-tests and t-tests shares one similarity: both of them are testing for the significance or the expected values of the coefficient estimates. In addition, when $J = 1$, the t- and F-tests are equivalent.

However, the two tests have several disparities:

1. In t-test, we have a hypothesis for testing a single estimated coefficient.
2. In an F-test we have joint hypotheses. F-test can also be used to perform a test on the significance of a model.
3. For the test with $a_k \neq 0$, the t-test is a two-tailed test whereas the F-test is a one-tailed test.
4. The F-distribution has J numerator degrees of freedom (df) and $(N - K)$ denominator df, whereas the t distribution has only one df for the numerator.

We are now ready to move to the next section.

Goodness-of-Fit and Reporting the Results

Goodness-of-Fit

An adjusted R^2 can measure the goodness-of-fit in multiple regression because using more than one variable decreases the degrees of freedom (df). As a result, the adjusted R^2 value is a better measure to account for the decreasing degrees of freedom, even though an R^2 value is still reported by most econometric packages, including Excel. The formula for calculating the adjusted R^2 value is:

$$Adjusted\ R^2 = \bar{R}^2 = 1 - \frac{SSE/(N-K)}{SST/(N-1)}. \tag{3.14}$$

In multiple regression, the concept of p-value learned in Chapter 2 comes very handy for measuring goodness-of-fit, because we might want to perform regression through the origin once in a while. Touro bursts out, "Yes, sometimes regressing with the intercept does not make sense. Yesterday, my boss wanted me to investigate how the sizes of land and buildings affect prices of vacation houses in the city. I ran a regression and found these results:

$$HOUSEP = 54,201 + 12\ LANDS + 102\ BUILDS,$$

where HOUSEP is the vacation-house prices, LANDS is the square feet of land, and BUILDS is the square feet of the building on the land. I stared at the results and told my boss that a house that has zero square feet of land costs roughly $54,000!"

Prof. Metric says that was an excellent example and that in this case, regressing through the origin makes more sense because the intercept should be zero; so, equation (3.3) becomes:

$$y_i = a_2 x_{i2} + \ldots + a_k x_{ik} + e_i. \tag{3.15}$$

The only problem is that R^2 value sometimes comes out negative, which is embarrassing, so using p-values to measure goodness-of-fit makes sense in this case.

Reporting the Results

We learn that the results for simple and multiple regression are reported in similar manners. The only difference between the two is that the adjusted R^2 is added for a multiple regression. For example:

$$SALE_i = 18.97 - 1.901\ PRICE_i + 0.763\ ADS_i;$$
$$(se)\quad (6.35)\quad\ (0.096)\ (0.314)$$
$$R^2 = 0.824;\ adjusted\ R^2 = 0.798;\ N = 36.$$

Data Analyses

Prof. Empirie says that a correlation analysis is crucial in multiple linear regression. Before estimating, we need to detect and eliminate any variable that causes multicollinearity.

Detecting Multicollinearity

The dataset is available in the file *Ch03.xls, Fig.3.1 to 3.2.* The dependent variable is investment (INV), and the two explanatory variables are tax credits by the government (CREDIT) and personal income (INCOME). First, we carry out a correlation analysis:

Go to Data then Data Analysis on the ribbon.
Select Correlation instead of Regression, then click OK.

A dialog box appears, as shown in Figure 3.1.

The result shows that the correlation coefficient between INCOME and CREDIT is 0.8016, which is acceptable to perform a regression (in the data file, you can find this correlation coefficient in cell Q3).

Regressing

Next, we perform a regression of INV on CREDIT and INCOME:

Go to Data then Data Analysis, select Regression and click OK.

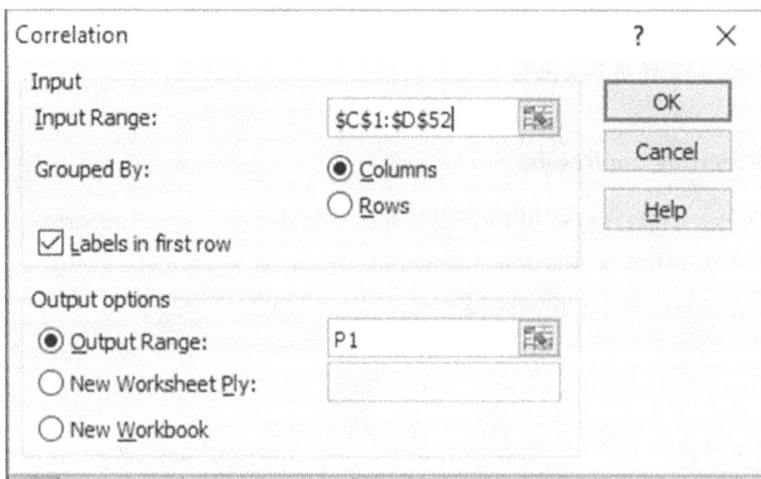

Figure 3.1 Dialog box for correlation analysis

The Input Y Range is B1:B52, the Input X Range is C1:D52.
Check the boxes Labels and Residuals.
Check the button Output Range and enter F1, then click OK.
A dialog box appears; click OK to overwrite the data.

We also copy and paste the correlation results into cells L1 though N3 together with the regression results in Figure 3.2, which shows the correlation coefficient in cell M3.

From these results, the estimated equation can be written as:

$$INV_i = -4421 + 0.1041 \ INCOME_i + 0.2592 \ CREDIT_i;$$
$$(se) \quad (1760) \ (0.0076) \ (0.0966)$$
$$R^2 = 0.9369; \text{ adjusted } R^2 = 0.9344.$$

Excel again displays the predicted values next to the residuals. Prof. Metric reminds us that we can use equations (3.8) and (3.9) to calculate interval prediction by following the steps given in Chapter 2.

Performing Regression for F-Tests

To carry out the F-test, we need to estimate two models: the unrestricted and the restricted. Data on Thailand-Japan real exchange rate (EXCHA), Real GDP (RGDP) for Thailand, and exports from Japan to Thailand (EXPS) are available in the file *Ch03.xls, Fig.3.3 to 3.4*. The hypothesis

								INCOME	CREDIT
SUMMARY OUTPUT									
							INCOME	1	
Regression Statistics							CREDIT	0.801577	1
Multiple R	0.967976491								
R Square	0.936978488								
Adjusted R Sq	0.934352591								
Standard Error	9355.305274								
Observations	51								
ANOVA									
	df	*SS*	*MS*	*F*	*Significance F*				
Regression	2	62459422365	31229711183	356.8223431	1.54075E-29				
Residual	48	4201043365	87521736.76						
Total	50	66660465730							
	Coefficients	*Standard Error*	*t Stat*	*P-value*	*Lower 95%*	*Upper 95%*	*ower 95.0%*	*pper 95.0%*	
Intercept	-4420.576144	1760.516816	-2.510953661	0.015461647	-7960.332445	-880.8198424	-7960.33	-880.82	
INCOME	0.104145050	0.007579745	13.73991644	2.96036E-18	0.088904959	0.119385154	0.088905	0.119385	
CREDIT	0.259240548	0.096588678	2.683964141	0.009954467	0.065035995	0.453445102	0.065036	0.453445	

Figure 3.2 Multiple regression results

is that EXCHA and RGDP jointly affect EXPS, so we regress $EXPS_t$ on $RGDP_t$ and $EXCHA_t$.

We learn that the following steps have to be performed:

Go to Data then Data Analysis, select Regression and click OK.
The input Y range is B1:B33, the input X range is C1:D33.
Check the box Labels.
Check the button Output Range and enter F1, then click OK.
A dialog box appears; click OK to overwrite the data.

The results for the unrestricted model are displayed in Figure 3.3. From these results, the estimated equation is:

$$EXPS_t = -970.0661 - 649.6924 \, EXCHA_t + 0.0193 \, RGDP_t,$$
$$SSE_U = 493,470,879.$$

We then estimate the restricted model by regressing $EXPS_t$ on $EXCHA_{t-1}$ using the same dataset:

Click Data and then Data Analysis on the ribbon.
Select Regression in the list and click OK.

	E	F	G	H	I	J	K	L	M
1		SUMMARY OUTPUT						EXCHAt	RGDPt
2		Regression Statistics					EXCHAt	1	
3		Multiple R	0.98612422				RGDPt	0.422599	1
4		R Square	0.972440977					(Ctrl) ▾	
5		Adjusted R Squ	0.970540355						
6		Standard Error	4125.074206						
7		Observations	32						
8		ANOVA							
9			df	SS	MS	F	gnificance F		
10		Regression	2	17412493434	8.71E+09	511.6435	2.42E-23		
11		Residual	29	493470879	17016237				
12		Total	31	17905964312					
13									
14			Coefficients	Standard Error	t Stat	P-value	Lower 95%	Upper 95%	
15		Intercept	-970.0660929	2844.64137	-0.34102	0.73555	-6788.01	4847.879	
16		EXCHAt	-649.6924223	436.4082004	-1.48873	0.147355	-1542.25	242.8626	
17		RGDPt	0.019323617	0.000653051	29.58975	3.24E-23	0.017988	0.020659	

H ◀ ▸ H | Fig.3.1-3.2 | Fig.3.3-3.4 | ℓℑ | ⃫ ◀ | ω | ▸ |

Figure 3.3 Estimation results for unrestricted model

Source: IMF Data and Statistics and the World Bank.

A dialog box appears.

Type B1:B33 into the Input Y Range box.

Type C1:C33 into the Input X Range box.

Choose Labels.

Check the Output Range button and enter F21.

Click OK.

A dialog box appears.

Click OK again to overwrite the data.

The estimated results are displayed in Figure 3.4. Prof. Empirie reminds us that we can also test for the model significance by using the unrestricted model with SST = 17,905,964,312 and the same SSE = 493,470,879.

From the results, the estimated equation is:

$$EXPS_t = -9929.6148 + 4807.4210 \ EXCHA_t,$$
$$SSE_R = 15,392.098,311.$$

Prof. Empirie also reminds us that there are two formulas for calculating F-statistics:

(i) The one for joint significance of the two coefficients uses SSE_U from the regression results in Figure 3.3 and the SSE_R from the regression results in Figure 3.4. The formula for calculating this F-statistic is in equation (3.11).

(ii) The F-test for the model significance only uses SST and SSE which come from the regression results in Figure 3.3. Hence, if the problem raised is to test for the model significance, we do not need to perform a regression on the restricted model. The formula for calculating this F-statistic is given in equation (3.13).

Invo suddenly exclaims, "Oh! In the regression of $EXPS_t$ on $RGDP_t$ and $EXCHA_t$, the two tests are the same because we have only two explanatory variables, so testing for the joint significance of these two variables is the same as testing for the model significance."

	E	F	G	H	I	J	K	L	M
19		SUMMARY OUTPUT							
20		Regression Statistics							
21		Multiple R	0.374690088						
22		R Square	0.140392662						
23		Adjusted R Squ	0.111739084						
24		Standard Error	22651.0473						
25		Observations	32						
26		ANOVA							
27			df	SS	MS	F	gnificance F		
28		Regression	1	2513866001	2.51E+09	4.899656	0.034609		
29		Residual	30	15392098311	5.13E+08				
30		Total	31	17905964312					
31									
32			Coefficients	Standard Error	t Stat	P-value	Lower 95%	Upper 95%	
33		Intercept	-9929.614766	15531.36747	-0.63933	0.527463	-41648.9	21789.67	
34		EXCHAt	4807.421043	2171.847788	2.213517	0.034609	371.9161	9242.926	

| | | | | | | | | | |
| H ◀ ▶ H | Fig.3.1-3.2 | Fig.3.3-3.4 | | | | | | | |

Figure 3.4 Estimation results for restricted model

Source: IMF Data and Statistics.

Prof. Empirie smiles, "Yes, that is very true."

We look at Invo with awe and are very happy that we need to practice performing only one test for the two cases when we get home.

Exercises

1. The file RGDP.xls contains data on real GDP (RGDP), consumption (CONS), investment (INV), and exports (EXPS). The data are for the United States, from the first quarter of 2006 to the first quarter of 2014. Given RGDP as the dependent variable,
   (a) Perform a correlation analysis for the three explanatory variables.
   (b) Perform a multiple regression of RGDP on the other three variables. Provide comments on the results, including the significances of a_1, a_2, and a_3, R^2, adjusted R^2, and the standard error of regression.

2. Write the estimated equation for the regression results for Exercise 1; enter the standard errors below the estimated coefficients, adding the adjusted R^2 next to the equation. Obtain the point prediction for the second quarter of the year 2014 based on this equation using a handheld calculator.

3. Use the results in Exercise 1 and carry out an additional regression on a restricted model as needed to test the joint significance of INV and EXPS at a 5 percent significance level. Write the procedure in four standard steps similar to those in the Hypothesis Testing section The calculations of the F-statistics may be performed using a hand-held calculator or using Excel.

PART II

Intermediate Topics

This part contains three chapters:

- Chapter 4 Simple Modeling Issues and Heteroscedasticity
- Chapter 5 Simple Dynamic Models and Autocorrelation
- Chapter 6 Panel Data Techniques

CHAPTER 4

Simple Modeling Issues and Heteroscedasticity

Today, Touro asks, "Prof. Metric, I heard that the linear regression technique only requires a model to be linear in parameters. What does that mean?" Booka then says, "I also have a question. In the previous chapters, we assumed that the data did not have any problems. What will happen if they violate one of the classic assumptions?" Prof. Metric praises them for raising good questions and tells us that several of these issues will be discussed this week. We learn that once we finish with the chapter, we will be able to:

1. Master simple model issues in regressions;
2. Explain the nature and consequences of the heteroscedasticity problem;
3. Obtain the corrected standard errors and the transformed models for estimations;
4. Carry out Excel applications to these models.

Functional Forms

Model Transformations

Prof. Metric explains that the "linear in parameters" requirement means that the model cannot have parameters in any nonlinear form, such as a_2^b. Other than that, the dependent and explanatory variables can be of any nonlinear form such as $Ln(Y)$ $Ln(X)$ $Ln(Y)$, $ln(X)$, or X^b. The reason is that we can easily transform a model that has nonlinear variables into a linear one. Equation 4.1 presents a logarithmic model with linear parameters:

$$Ln\ Y = a_1 + a_2\ Ln(X). \tag{4.1}$$

We can transform this model by letting $Y^* = Ln(Y)$ and letting $X^* = Ln(X)$; then, the model becomes a linear one:

$$Y^* = a_1 + a_2\ X^*.$$

Similarly, a polynomial model

$$Y = a_1 + a_2\ X^2 + a_3\ Z^3 \tag{4.2}$$

can be transformed by letting $X^* = X^2$, and $Z^* = Z^3$; then the model also becomes a linear one in parameters:

$$Y = a_1 + a_2\ X^* + a_3\ Z^*.$$

These transformations allow us to employ OLS estimation techniques using Excel, as usual.

Choosing a Logarithmic Model

The following log models are the most important in data analysis, and we want to learn how to interpret them.

Log-Log Model

This model is written as:

$$\ln y_i = a_1 + a_2 \ln x_i + e_i. \tag{4.3}$$

In this case, the parameter a_2 measures the elasticity of y with respect to x.

For example, the following model measures the price elasticity of demand:

$$\ln DEMAND_i = a_1 + a_2 \ln PRICE_i + e_i.$$

Booka raises her hand and offers her estimation for the price elasticity of demand for history books at her company. The estimation is based on her recent survey. The estimation results are:

$$\ln DEMAND_i = 0.3 - 1.1 \ln PRICE_i.$$

Invo offers "So, a 1 percent increase in the price of your history books decreases the demand for these books by 1.1 percent." Touro adds, "Oh, the demand for your history books is slightly elastic because its price elasticity is a little greater than 1. You might want to draw several more samples to see whether the results are robust to sample changes. If this is true, your company might want to lower the prices slightly to boost sales." Prof. Metric praises them for an insightful discussion and moves to the next section.

Log-Linear Model

This model is written as:

$$\ln y_i = a_1 + a_2 x_i + e_i. \tag{4.4a}$$

In this case, the slope a_2 measures the percent change ($a_2 \times 100$) in y due to a one-unit change in x.

For example, the following model measures the impact of investing in new capital on the profit of a company:

$$\ln PROFIT_i = a_1 + a_2 CAPITAL_i + e_i.$$

Taila says that her company bought several new machines six months ago and found their effect on the company's monthly profit as follows:

$$\ln PROFIT_i = a_1 + 0.02 CAPITAL_i,$$

where CAPITAL was measured in thousands of dollars.

We are able to calculate the impact of this change in capital on the profit as $\Delta PROFIT = (0.02*100)\% = 2\%$. Since the unit of capital is in thousands of dollars, this 2 percent change in profit is due to a $1,000 increase in capital.

Linear-Log Model

This model is written as:

$$y_i = a_1 + a_2 \ln x_i + e_i. \tag{4.4b}$$

In this case, a 1 percent change in x leads to a $(a_2/100)$ unit change in y.

Touro offers an example model, in which spending depends on log of income:

$$SPEND_i = a_1 + a_2 \ln(INCOME)_i + e_i.$$

Prof. Metric says this is an interesting case: if $a_2 > 0$, an increase in income will cause an increase in spending, indicating that the good is a normal good, but the log function also implies that spending will increase at a decreasing rate, because the graph of a log function is concave with a decreasing slope. Touro says this is the case with spending on travel at his company, where the result for regression is:

$$SPEND_i = 200 + 1400 \ln(INCOME)_i + e_i,$$

where the unit of spending (SPEND) is in thousands of dollars.

We can calculate the impact of the change in income on the spending for travel, for Touro, as ΔSPEND = (1400/100) = 14. Since the unit of spending is in thousands of dollars, we conclude that a 1 percent change in income causes a $14,000 change in travel spending at Touro's company.

Growth Rate

Prof. Metric reminds us that $\ln(1+x) \cong x$ if x is small (less than 20 percent) and that we learned this approximation in algebra classes. This formula can have practical applications here. Invo offers an example on the growth of revenue from his company, where they found this equation related to revenue over time:

$$REVENUE_t = (1 + r) REVENUE_{t-1}, \qquad (4.5)$$

where r is the yearly growth rate of revenue.

We are able to go back to the first period as follows:

$$REVENUE_t = REVENUE_0 (1 + r)^t.$$

Taking the logarithms of both sides yields:

$$\ln(REVENUE_t) = \ln(REVENUE_o) + \left[\ln(1 + r)\right] \times t.$$

Let $\ln(RETURN_0) = a_1$ and $[\ln(1 + r)] = a_2$, then

$$\ln(REVENUE_t) = a_1 + a_2 t.$$

Invo provides us with the following estimation results:

$$\ln(REVENUE) = 0.2413 + 0.0276 \times t.$$

We are able to write the approximation as:

$$\left[\ln(1 + r)\right] \approx r = (0.0276 * 100)\% = 2.76\%.$$

Hence, the growth rate of revenue at Invo's company is approximately 2.76 percent per year.

Return to Training

Prof. Metric says that we can similarly have wages as a function of training, so:

$$\ln(WAGE)_t = \ln(WAGE_0) + \left[\ln(1 + r)\right] \times TRAINING_{t-1}, \quad (4.6)$$

$$\ln(WAGE) = a_1 + a_2 TRAINING_{t-1},$$

where r is rate of return to an extra month of training.

Suppose the estimation result is:

$$\ln\left(WAGE\right)_t = 0.4315 + 0.0124 * TRAINING_{t-1},$$

then an additional month of training increases the wage rate by approximately 1.24 percent.

Prof. Metric reminds us that all log models can be extended to multiple regressions by adding more control variables, as discussed in Chapter 3, or by adding dummy variables, as will be discussed in the following section.

Intercept Dummy Variables

Additive Dummy Variables

An intercept dummy is called an additive dummy because this variable is added to the model. We can add dummy variables (also called indicator variables) to a model to control for the difference in characteristics among various groups. Prof. Metric tells us to go back to Booka's example of the paperback or hardback books. The original model on their sale values can be written as follows:

$$SALE_i = a_1 + a_2 INCOME_i + e_i. \tag{4.7}$$

Let $D = 1$ if the book is in paperback and $D = 0$ otherwise, then we have two groups in this case (numbers of groups = $G = 2$). Suppose the dataset has 15 observations for $D = 1$ and 15 observations for $D = 0$, then the dummy-variable method has two advantages:

(i) It allows us to use the whole dataset of 30 observations.

(ii) We can compare and contrast the difference between the two groups.

Prof. Metric says that we can have more than two groups—for example, cars can come in green, red, blue, or brown, and thus $G = 4$.

In the aforementioned example on book sales, if we add D to equation (4.7), then

$$SALE_i = a_1 + a_2 INCOME_i + dD_i + e_i. \tag{4.8}$$

$$\text{Then } E(SALE) \begin{cases} = (a_1 + d) + a_2 INCOME \text{ if } D = 1 \\ = a_1 + a_2 INCOME \text{ if } D = 0 \end{cases}. \tag{4.9}$$

The intercept might not have any meaning, but the difference in the intercepts depicts the differences in the prices for different type of books. Suppose $d = -15$, and $SALE$ is in dollars, then a paperback copy reduces the sale value by $15.

To choose the reference group, a researcher can only add $(G\text{-}1)$ dummies in the regression. For example, for two groups, use one dummy. Otherwise, the sum of D_1 and D_2 equals 1. Since the coefficient estimate for the constant terms is a vector of all 1s, we will have a perfect-collinearity problem if we add G dummies. This problem is also called the dummy-variable trap.

Heteroscedasticity

Nature and Consequences

In the previous chapters, we assumed that the errors have a constant variance, var$(e_i) = \sigma^2$. Prof. Metric says that when this variance is not constant, then the classic assumption (*iii*) is violated, and the errors are said to be heteroskedastic. To see the problem, we all look at the original equation:

$$y_i = a_1 + a_2 x_i + e_i. \tag{4.10}$$

If var$(e_i) = \sigma_i^2$ (note the subscript i), the variance changes when the identity changes, and we have a heteroscedasticity problem.

For example, if $\sigma_i^2 = \sigma^2 \sqrt{x_i}$, where $\sigma^2 = 100$ and the variable x_i changes from $64 to $81, then we can obtain

$$\sigma_1^2 = \sigma^2 \sqrt{x_1} = 100 * 8 = 800.$$

But $\sigma_2^2 = \sigma^2 \sqrt{x_2} = 100 * 9 = 900.$

Thus, the error variance, σ_i^2, changes from 800 to 900 instead of remaining a constant. The heteroscedasticity problem could occur with time-series data as well.

To this point, Invo says, "Oh yes, suppose we want to perform a regression of food expenditures on income, then the variance of errors might change because this variance might be correlated with income as well."

Touro asks, "How come the variance of the errors is correlated with income?" Invo answers, "Because food expenditures also depend on the price level, which in turn might go up if income goes up. Since price is not included in the model, it must be contained in the error term. As a result, the variance of the errors is correlated with income."

Prof. Metric praises Invo and says that there are two consequences of heteroscedasticity:

(i) The standard errors are incorrect, so statistical inferences are not reliable.

(ii) The OLS estimator is no longer the BLUE, so its variance is not the smallest.

Each problem can be addressed separately, and we will learn how to overcome them in the next section.

Detecting Heteroscedasticity

A Lagrange Multiplier (LM) test is usually performed to test a variance function so that we can find out if a heteroscedasticity problem exists. The theoretical foundation behind this test is simple. Given the model in equation (4.10) with $\text{var}(e_i) = \sigma_i^2$, we let the error variance be a function of a variable w:

$$\text{var}(e_i) = \sigma_i^2 = E(e_i^2) = f(c_1 + c_2 w). \qquad (4.11)$$

We then test for the significance of c_2. Since c_1 is a constant, if c_2 is not statistically different from zero, then $\text{var}(e) = c_1 = $ a constant, so the hypotheses are:

$$H_0: c_2 = 0; H_a: c_2 \neq 0.$$

We learn that there are several LM tests. In this lecture, Prof. Metric teaches us the White version, which is the most popular one and which has $w = x$. The test utilizes the chi-squared distribution, $\chi^2_{(K-1)}$, where K is the number of estimated coefficients (parameters), and $(K - 1)$ is the degrees of freedom (df). Here are the steps to perform this LM test:

First, we need to estimate the original equation: $y_i = a_1 + a_2 x_i + e_i$.

Next, we obtain $\hat{e}_i$ and generate $\hat{e}_i^2$ so that we can estimate the variance function:

$$\hat{e}_i^2 = c_1 + c_2 x_i + v_i. \tag{4.12}$$

After that, we can follow the four-step procedure for any test:

(i) $H_0: c_2 = 0; H_a: c_2 \neq 0.$
(ii) Calculate $LM_{STAT} = N*R^2.$ $\hspace{2cm}$ (4.13)
(iii) Find $\chi^2_c = \chi^2_{(K-1)}$ either using a chi-squared distribution table or by typing $=CHIINV(\alpha, df)$ in any Excel cell, where the degrees of freedom is $K - 1$, which is 1 in this case.
(iv) If $LM_{STAT} > \chi^2_C$, we reject the null hypothesis, meaning c_2 is different from zero and implying that heteroskedasticity exists.

Prof. Metric then gives us an example, "Let's say estimating $\hat{e}_i^2 = c_1 + c_2 x_i + v_i$ yields $R^2 = 0.25$ and the sample size is $N = 30$; how can we perform the LM test?"

We work out the problem together by calculating:

$LM_{STAT} = 30*0.25 = 7.5$ for $\alpha = 0.05$; the critical value of $\chi^2_{(2-1)}$ is 3.84.

Hence, we reject the null, meaning that c_2 is different from zero and implying that the data has a heteroskedasticity problem.

We can also type $=CHIINV(0.05, 1)$ into an Excel cell and see that Excel reports the critical value as $3.8415 \approx 3.84$.

Correcting Heteroscedasticity

Since there are two possible consequences with heteroscedasticity, we can discuss each of them separately.

(i) *The standard errors are incorrect*

If the form of the heteroscedasticity is unknown, OLS can be used to estimate the coefficients. Then, corrected variances are calculated using the robust standard error method introduced by White (1980) and so also called White's standard errors.

Theoretically, White's variance and standard error for a_2 are:

$$\text{var}(a_2) = \frac{\sum\left[(x_i - \bar{x})^2 \sigma_i^2\right]}{\left[\sum(x_i - \bar{x})^2\right]^2}. \tag{4.14}$$

Empirically,

$$\hat{\text{var}}(a_2) = \frac{\sum\left[(x_i - \bar{x})^2 \hat{e}_i^2\right]}{\left[\sum(x_i - \bar{x})^2\right]^2}; \quad se(a_2) = \sqrt{\hat{\text{var}}(b_2)}. \tag{4.15}$$

We are happy to hear that we do not have to calculate this White's standard error because we will learn how to obtain it using Excel later in this chapter.

(ii) *The OLS estimator is no longer the BLUE*

Since the OLS estimator is no longer the BLUE, when we have a heteroscedasticity problem it is better if we can find an alternative estimator with a smaller variance. When the form of the heteroscedasticity is known, we can find a generalized least squares (GLS) estimator to replace the OLS estimator. There are several approaches to GLS estimations. Given the model in equation (4.1), we first study the simplest one by assuming that $\sigma_i^2 = \sigma^2 x_i$. In this case we must divide both sides of the equation (4.1) by $\sqrt{x_i}$:

$$y_1^* = \frac{y_i}{\sqrt{x_i}}; \, x_{i1}^* = \frac{1}{\sqrt{x_i}}; \, x_{i2}^* = \frac{x_i}{\sqrt{x_i}}; \, e_i^* = \frac{e_i}{\sqrt{x_i}}. \tag{4.16}$$

Then we perform a regression on the transformed equation:

$$y_i^* = a_1 x_{i1}^* + a_2 x_2^* + e_i^*.   \tag{4.17}$$

Touro exclaims, "Oh, this model no longer has a constant variable, because x_{i1}^* changes with each observation." Prof. Metric says that is true, so we need to suppress the constant when performing the regression and that Prof. Empirie will show us how to do it in Excel.

He then says that the problem is solved, because

$$\text{var}\left(e_i^*\right) = \text{var}\left(\frac{e_i}{\sqrt{x_i}}\right) = \frac{1}{x_i}\text{var}\left(e_i\right) = \frac{1}{x_i}\sigma^2 x_i = \sigma^2.$$

We also learn that the predicted values reported in Excel are for y^*, so we need to multiply $\hat{y}^*$ by $\sqrt{x_i}$ to obtain the predicted value for $\hat{y}$. The interval prediction values then can be calculated as usual.

Prof. Metric tells us that sometimes the form of heteroscedasticity is much more complex, so transforming the model by $\sqrt{x_i}$ does not correct the problem. In practice, we don't know the form of the heteroscedasticity, so we have to estimate a more general form.

We are excited and say in unison, "Let's learn a more general case," and Prof. Metric introduces this model:

$$\text{Let } \text{var}\left(e_i\right) = \sigma_i^2 = \sigma^2 x_i^{\gamma}.$$

Theoretically, $\ln(\sigma_i^2) = \ln(\sigma^2) + \gamma(\ln x_i)$, so we can find σ_i^2 by performing a regression of this equation.

Empirically, we don't have σ^2, so we need to run a regression on $y_i = a_1 + a_2 x_i + e_i$ and obtain $\hat{e}_i$. After that, we need to obtain estimate values of $\ln(\sigma^2)$ and $g(\ln x_i)$ by writing the relation as:

$$\ln\left(\hat{e}_i^2\right) = \ln\left(\sigma_i^2\right) + v_i = \alpha_1 + \alpha_2 z_i + v_i,   \tag{4.18}$$

where $\alpha_1 = \ln\left(\sigma^2\right)$; $\alpha_2 = \gamma$; $z_i = \ln x_i$.

Therefore, the estimated version of equation (4.18) is:

$$\ln(\hat{\sigma}_i^2) = \ln(\hat{\hat{e}}_i^2) = \hat{\alpha}_1 + \hat{\alpha}_2 z_i.   \tag{4.19}$$

From equation (4.19), we can calculate the estimated variance:

$$\hat{\sigma}_i^2 = \exp\left(\hat{a}_1 + \hat{a}_2 z_i \right). \tag{4.20}$$

Next, we can make the transformation:

$$y_i^* = \frac{y_i}{\hat{\sigma}_i}; \quad x_{i1}^* = \frac{1}{\hat{\sigma}_i}; \quad x_{i2}^* = \frac{x_i}{\hat{\sigma}_i}; \quad e_i^* = \frac{e_i}{\hat{\sigma}_i}. \tag{4.21}$$

Then we can estimate $y_i^* = a_1 x_{i1}^* + a_2 x_{i2}^* + e_i^*$. $\qquad$ (4.22)

The problem is solved, because

$$\text{var}\left(e_i^*\right) = \text{var}\left(\frac{e_i}{\sigma_i}\right) = \frac{1}{\sigma_i^2}\text{var}\left(e_i\right) = \frac{1}{\sigma_i^2}\sigma_i^2 = 1.$$

Prof. Metric says the correction can also be extended to multiple regressions. In this case, the formula for calculating the estimated variance is:

$$\hat{\sigma}_i^2 = \exp\left(\hat{a}_1 + \hat{a}_2 z_{i2} + ... + \hat{a}_K z_{iK} \right),$$

where K is the number of parameters.

Data Analyses

Prof. Empirie reminds us that the Chow test is similar to the F-tests discussed in Chapter 3, in which she already showed us how to estimate the unrestricted and restricted models. Moreover, adding dummy variables to a regression is just like adding any variable. Hence, in this section she only provides instructions for heteroscedasticity.

Detecting Heteroscedasticity

The yearly data on spending (SPEND) and salary (SAL) are available in the file *Ch04.xls. Fig.4.1*, and a section of the second regression with the N and R^2 is shown in Figure 4.1. First, we regress SPEND on SAL.

Click Data and then Data Analysis on the ribbon.

Select Regression, then click OK.

Type B1:B34 into the Input Y Range box.

Type A1:A34 into the Input X Range box.

Choose Labels and Residuals.

Check the Output Range button and enter F1.

Click OK then OK again to override the data range.

Copy and paste the residuals (*e*) from cells H24 through H57 into cells C1 through C34.

To generate e-squared (e^2), type =*C2^2* into cell D2, then press Enter.

Copy and paste this formula into cells D3 through D34.

Next, we need to regress e^2 on SAL.

Click Data and then Data Analysis on the ribbon.

Select Regression, then click OK.

Enter D1:D34 into the Input Y Range box.

Enter A1:A34 into the Input X Range box.

Choose Labels.

Check the Output Range button and enter P1.

Click OK then OK again to override the data range.

From Figure 4.1, $N = 33$ and $R^2 = 0.1913$, so $LM_{STAT} = 33*0.1913 = 6.31$.

Typing =*CHIINV(0.05,1)* into any Excel cell gives you $\chi_c^2 = \chi_{(2-1)}^2 = 3.84$.

Since $LM_{STAT} > \chi_c^2$, we reject the null hypothesis, meaning the coefficient of the residuals $\hat{v}$ is statistically different from zero, implying that the model has a heteroscedasticity problem.

M	O	P	Q	R	S	T	
1	SUMMARY OUTPUT						
2							
3	*Regression Statistics*						
4	Multiple R	0.437399721					
5	R Square	0.191318516					
6	Adjusted R Square	0.165232017					
7	Standard Error	5562904.989					
8	Observations	33					
9							
10	ANOVA						
11		*df*	*SS*	*MS*	*F*	*Significance F*	

Figure 4.1 **R^2 and N for testing heteroscedasticity**

Correcting Heteroscedasticity

Obtaining White's Standard Error

Prof. Empirie has utilized the results from the first regression for Figure 4.1, and we find them in the file *Ch04.xls, Fig.4.2*. We learn to perform the following steps:

> In cell E2 type =AVERAGE(A2:A34), then press Enter (this is Xbar).
> In cell F2 type =(A2 – E2)^2, then press Enter (this is $(X - Xbar)^2$).
> In cell G2 type =F2*D2, then press Enter (this is the numerator, NUMER, in the data file).
> Copy and paste the formulas in cells F2 and G2 down the columns.
> In cell F35 type =SUM(F2:F34), then press Enter.
> In cell G35 type =SUM(G2:G34), then press Enter.
> In cell G36 type =G35/(F35^2), then press Enter (this is the corrected var (a_2)).
> In cell G37 type =SQRT(G36), then press Enter (this is the corrected se (a_2)).

The results are reported in Figure 4.2 with the corrected $var(a_2) = 0.0006$ and $se(a_2) = 0.0238$.

Estimating a Transformed Model

The yearly data on SPEND and SAL are used again in this demonstration and are available in the file *Ch04.xls, Fig.4.3*. We learn to perform the following steps:

> In cell C2 type =A2^1/2), then press Enter (this is $SAL^{1/2}$).

	A	B	C	D	E	F	G	H
29	46729.8	4777.74	772.2381	596351.8		2241662.284	1.33682E+12	
30	58267.8	5057.6	956.1818	914283.6		169916913	1.55352E+14	
31	49503.6	5097.51	1068.901	1142550		18241596.31	2.08419E+13	
32	19747.8	5103.78	1323.05	1750460		649474104.3	1.13688E+15	
33	64654.2	5266.8	1111.98	1236500		377199252.8	4.66407E+14	
34	36271.8	5329.5	1411.118	1991253		80295610.79	1.59889E+14	
35						7691299128	3.3512E+16	
36						White var (a₂)	0.000566502	
37						White se (a₂)	0.0238013	

Fig.4.1 Fig.4.2 Fig.4.3

Figure 4.2 Obtaining white's standard error for a_2

Copy and paste the formula into cells C3 through C34.
In cell D2 type =B2/C2 (this is SPEND*).
Copy and paste the formula into cells D3 through D34.
In cell E2 type =1/C2 (this is X1*).
Copy and paste the formula into cells E3 through E34.
In cell F2 type =A2/C2 (this is SAL*).
Copy and paste the formula into cells F3 through F34.

Next, we need to regress SPEND* on X1* and SAL*'.

Go to Data Analysis and choose Regression.
Type D1:D34 into the Input Y Range box.
Type E1:F34 into the Input X Range box.
Check the box Labels; Constant is Zero.
(Make sure that you suppress the constant because the model no longer has a constant.)
Check the Output Range button and enter H1.
Click OK then OK again to obtain the regression results.

The regression results for the transformed model are displayed in Figure 4.3.

Prof. Empirie reminds us that to obtain the predicted value for SPEND*, we just need to check the box Residuals when we enter the

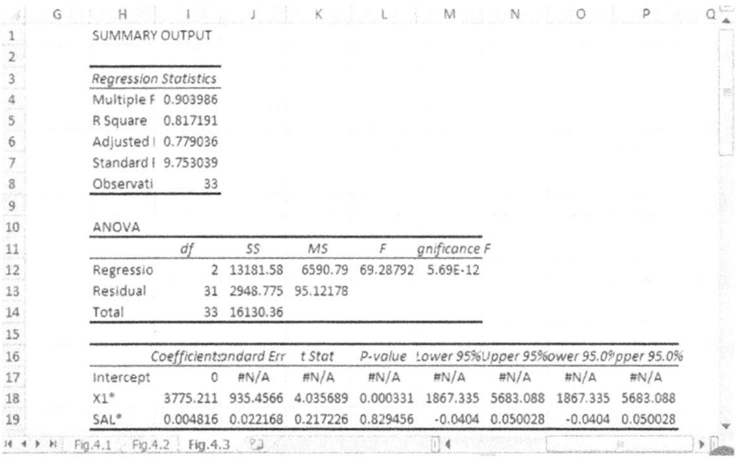

SUMMARY OUTPUT

Regression Statistics	
Multiple F	0.903986
R Square	0.817191
Adjusted I	0.779036
Standard I	9.753039
Observati	33

ANOVA

	df	SS	MS	F	gnificance F
Regressio	2	13181.58	6590.79	69.28792	5.69E-12
Residual	31	2948.775	95.12178		
Total	33	16130.36			

	Coefficient:	andard Err	t Stat	P-value	Lower 95%	Upper 95%	ower 95.0%	pper 95.0%
Intercept	0	#N/A	#N/A	#N/A	#N/A	#N/A	#N/A	#N/A
X1*	3775.211	935.4566	4.035689	0.000331	1867.335	5683.088	1867.335	5683.088
SAL*	0.004816	0.022168	0.217226	0.829456	-0.0404	0.050028	-0.0404	0.050028

Figure 4.3 Regression results for the transformed model

regression commands so that Excel will report them in its Summary Output. However, we still need to multiply predicted SPEND* by SAL$^{1/2}$ to obtain the predicted SPEND. The interval prediction values can then be calculated as usual.

Exercises

1. The yearly data on earning (EARN) and capital (CAP) are available in the file Capital.xls. Regress CAP on EARN using Excel and obtain the residuals $\hat{e}$. Use the results to perform the heteroscedasticity test for the model.

2. Propose two alternative methods to correct the heteroscedasticity problem in Question 1.

3. The estimation results of a model are listed in Table 4.1. The dependent variable is $ln(price)$ with price in dollars and the independent variables are areas of the houses in square feet ($sqft$) and an intercept dummy: $D_1 = 1$ if a house is in the volcano area ($volcan$) and 0 otherwise. Provide an interpretation of $volcan$, including the meaning, magnitude, and significant level of the estimated coefficient.

Table 4.1 Estimation results for exercise 3

	Coefficients	Standard error	p-value
Intercept	4.0536	1.1165	0.006
Sqft	0.0671	0.0203	0.008
Volcan	−0.1056	−0.0329	0.009

CHAPTER 5

Simple Dynamic Models in Time-Series Data

Having learned about heteroscedasticity, Touro was wondering what particular problems could occur with time-series data. Prof. Metric commends him for a good question and says that we will discuss these problems in this chapter and will be able to:

1. Detect the autocorrelation in time-series data and master the corrections;
2. Analyze the autoregressive models and applications;
3. Explain other dynamic models and perform the relevant tests;
4. Apply Excel into estimating the models learned in (1), (2), and (3).

Prof. Metric says that dynamic models examine the continuous impact of any change over more than one period. We will examine the effect in three ways: lag values of the error, lag values of the dependent variables, and lag values of the explanatory variables.

Autocorrelation

Prof. Metric says that a static model for time-series data contains only variables of the contemporaneous period for all explanatory and dependent variables. In this case, if all classic assumptions are also satisfied, then regression of time-series data is similar to that of cross-sectional data; that is, OLS produces BLUE results. Thus, this static model does not need any correction before running a regression, and the simple-regression model is written as:

$$y_t = a_1 + a_2 + e_t, \tag{5.1}$$

where $Cov(e_t, e_z) = 0$ for $t \neq z$.

Or, for multiple regressions:

$$y_t = a_1 + a_2 x_{2t} + \ldots + a_k x_{kt} + e_t, \tag{5.2}$$

where $\text{Cov}(e_t, e_z) = 0$ for $t \neq z$.

Prof. Metric reminds us that we already had hands-on experience in Chapter 3 performing a regression of $EXPS_t$ on $RGDP_t$ and $EXCHA_t$.

However, if the classic assumption (*iv*) for time series $\text{Cov}(e_t, e_z) = 0$ for $t \neq z$ is violated even when all explanatory and dependent variables are in the current period—that is, $\text{Cov}(e_t, e_z) \neq 0$ for $t \neq z$—then we have a dynamic model with lag values of the error, and the problem is called autocorrelation or serial correlation. Given equation (5.1), the autocorrelation equations with one lag error and k lag errors are written respectively as:

$$e_t = re_{t-1} + v_t; \tag{5.3a}$$

$$e_t = r_1 e_{t-1} + r_2 e_{t-2} + \ldots + r_k e_{t-k} + v_t. \tag{5.3b}$$

Combining equation (5.3a) or equation (5.3b) with equation (5.1) yields the following model for one lag error or k lag errors, respectively:

$$y_t = a_1 + a_2 x_t + re_{t-1} + v_t; \tag{5.4a}$$

$$y_t = a_1 + a_2 x_t + r_1 e_{t-1} + r_2 e_{t-2} + \ldots + r_k e_{t-k} + v_t. \tag{5.4b}$$

In equations (5.4a) and (5.4b), v_t has a constant variance

$$\sigma_v^2 \text{ and } \text{cov}(v_t, v_z) = 0; \; t \neq z.$$

We also assume that all series are stationary, $|r_k| < 1$ for $k = 1, 2, \ldots, k$.

In addition, it can be shown that

$$E(e_t) = 0; \quad \text{var}(e_t) = \sigma_e^2 = \left(\sigma_v^2\right) / \left(1 - r^2\right).$$

Hence, e_t is also homoscedastic.

However, the covariance of e_t and e_{t-k} is not homoscedastic. Specifically, it can be shown that

$$\text{cov}\left(e_t, e_{t-k}\right) = \sigma_e^2 r^k.$$

From these results, the population correlation function is:

$$\text{corr}\left(e_t, e_{t-k}\right) = \frac{\text{cov}\left(e_t, e_{t-k}\right)}{\sqrt{\text{var}\left(e_t\right)}\sqrt{\text{var}\left(e_{t-k}\right)}} = \frac{\text{cov}\left(e_t, e_{t-k}\right)}{\sqrt{\sigma_e^2}\sqrt{\sigma_e^2}} = \frac{\sigma_e^2 r^k}{\sigma_e^2} = r^k. \quad (5.5)$$

Since (5.4a) has only one lag value of the errors, $k = 1$, and $corr(e_t, e_{t-1}) = r$.

Equations (5.4a) and (5.4b) and (5.5) tell us that there are certain relations between the error terms of two or more periods, so the model has an autocorrelation problem.

Prof. Metric says that the two consequences of the autocorrelation are similar to those of heteroscedasticity:

(i) The standard errors are incorrect, so statistical inferences are not reliable.
(ii) The OLS estimator is still unbiased, but it is no longer the BLUE, so it is possible to find an alternative estimator with a lower variance.

Also, similar to heteroscedasticity, the correction for each problem will be discussed separately in the next section.

Detecting Autocorrelation

We learn that we can examine an autocorrelation function or carry out an LM test to detect autocorrelation.

Autocorrelation Function

The series r_k, where $k = 1, 2,..., k$, is called the autocorrelation function or the correlogram of the errors. This function reveals the correlation between the errors that are two periods apart through k periods apart. The estimated correlation function, which is a sample version of equation (5.5) is:

$$\hat{r}_k = \left(\sum_{t=k+1}^{T} \hat{e}_t \, \hat{e}_{t-k} \right) / \sum_{t=k+1}^{T} \hat{e}_{t-k}^2. \qquad (5.6)$$

Thus, we can perform a regression of equation (5.2), obtain the residual $\hat{e}_t$, and generate thee lag values of $\hat{e}_t$ so that we can calculate each $\hat{r}_k$. We then compare this $\hat{r}_k$ with the ratio $\pm 1.96 \, / \, T^{1/2}$, similar to equation (1.15). The value ± 1.96 is the 95 percent bounds of a standard normal distribution, and T is the sample size. We will reject the null hypothesis of no autocorrelation if

$$\left| \hat{r}_k \right| > \left(1.96 \, / \, T^{1/2} \right).$$

In this case, one or more lag error terms are correlated to the current error term, implying that the autocorrelation problem exists.

Booka asks, "Why do we have to use $t = k+1$ in equation (5.6)?" Taila offers an explanation,

Once we obtain the residual $\hat{e}_t$ from regression, we need to generate its lag values. For example, if you want to test the model in equation (5.4a), then $k = 1$. In this case, we need to generate e_{t-1} and will lose the first observation. Hence, the sum in equation (5.6) will start from $t = 2$ because $k + 1 = 1 + 1 = 2$. For $k = 2$, the sum will have to start from $t = 3$, and so on.

Prof. Metric is very pleased with Taila's explanation and says that we will have a chance to practice this method in the Exercises section. Most econometric software programs provide a graph of the correlogram with the bounds $\pm \, 1.96 \, / \, T^{1/2}$, called the 95 percent Bartlett Band, superimposed on the graph so that we do not have to calculate it by hand. The terminology "Barlett Band" comes from a seminal work on this subject by Bartlett (1946). For Excel, we will have to buy an Add-in tool called NumXL, so Prof. Metric does not require us to draw this graph.

LM Test

We focus on the case with one lag error first. The empirical version of equation (5.4a) contains $\hat{e}_{t-1}$ and $\hat{v}_t$:

$$y_t = a_1 + a_2 x_t + r\hat{e}_{t-1} + \hat{v}_t, \text{ but}$$

$$y_t = \hat{a}_1 + \hat{a}_2 x_t + \hat{e}_t, \text{ so}$$

$$\hat{a}_1 + \hat{a}_2 + x_t + \hat{e}_t = a_1 + a_2 x_t + r\hat{e}_{t-1} + \hat{v}_t$$

$$\hat{e}_t = \left(a_1 - \hat{a}_1\right) + \left(a_2 - \hat{a}_2\right)x_t + r\hat{e}_{t-1} + \hat{v}_t,$$

$$\hat{e}_t = c_1 + c_2 x + r\hat{e}_{t-1} + \hat{v}_t, \qquad (5.7)$$

where $c_1 = a_1 - \hat{a}_1$ and $c_2 = a_2 - \hat{a}_2$,

Hence, the procedure for performing the LM test for (5.4a) is as follows.

Estimate the model equation (5.1): $y_t = a_1 + a_2 + e_t$.
Obtain $\hat{e}_t$ and generate $\hat{e}_{t-1}$

Estimate equation (5.7) and obtain R^2 for the four-step LM test:

(i) $H_0: r = 0; H_a: r \neq 0$.
(ii) Calculate $LM_{STAT} = T*R^2$.
(iii) Find $\chi_c^2 = \chi_{(J)}^2$ using either a chi-square distribution table or Excel.
    Note that J is the degree of freedom and equals the number of restrictions; in this case J = 1 because we only have to test one lag value for e_{t-1}.
(iv) If $LM_{STAT} > \chi_c^2$ we reject the null hypothesis, meaning r is different from zero and implying that autocorrelation exists.

Next, Prof. Metric gives us an example, "Suppose estimating the model in equation (5.7) yields $R^2 = 0.205$, and the sample size $T = 24$, then what is the test results?"
We work on the test as follows:

(i) $H_0: r = 0; H_a: r \neq 0$.
(ii) Calculate $LM_{STAT} = T*R^2 = 24*0.205 = 4.92$.
(iii) Find $\chi_c^2 = \chi_{(J)}^2$: we try both a chi-square distribution table and Excel, and find that $\chi_{(1)}^2 = 3.84$.

(iv) Since $LM_{STAT} > \chi_c^2$, we reject the null hypothesis, meaning r is different from zero and implying that autocorrelation exists.

Prof. Metric says that the test can be extended to equation (5.4b) in the same manner except that J will be equal to the number of lag errors that need to be tested.

Correcting Autocorrelation

(i) *The standard errors are incorrect*

Similar to the case of heteroscedasticity, OLS can be used to estimate the coefficients when autocorrelation is present, and then corrected standard errors are computed. The corrected standard errors are called the heteroscedasticity and autocorrelation consistent (HAC) or Newey-West standard errors. The concept of HAC standard errors is similar to that of White's standard errors introduced in the previous chapter.

Nevertheless, Newey-West standard errors are superior to White's standard errors in two regards: first, they correct for both problems, heteroskedasticity and autocorrelation; second, they are consistent for autocorrelated errors in all forms and so do not require a specification of a dynamic error model as in the case of the heteroscedasticity problem. Ignoring autocorrelation often leads to overstating the reliability of the OLS estimates.

For example, estimating a model with autocorrelation yields the following results:

$$y_1 = 4.74 + 2.48x_t; \quad R^2 = 0.88; T = 56.$$
(se) (2.37) (1.02)   incorrect standard error
(se) (3.65) (1.97)   correct standard error

Hence, the t-tests using incorrect standard errors give significant coefficient estimates while the correct ones yield insignificant ones.

(ii) *The OLS estimator is no longer the BLUE*

Although the corrected standard errors can be obtained, we learn that it is preferable to use another form of the GLS models to obtain an estimator that is BLUE when an autocorrelation problem exists. Given the following model:

$$y_t = a_1 + a_2 x_t + e_t \text{ and } e_t = re_{t-1} + v_1, \text{ we have}$$

$$y_t = a_1 + a_2 x_t + re_{t-1} + v_t.$$

Retrogress backward one period:

$$y_{t-1} = a_1 + a_2 x_{t-1} + \hat{e}_{t-1},$$

so

$$\hat{e}_{t-1} = y_{t-1} - a_1 - a_2 x_t$$

$$y_t = a_1 + a_2 x_t + r\left(y_{t-1} - a_1 - a_2 x_{t-1}\right) + v_t$$

$$= a_1 + a_2 x_t + ry_{t-1} - ra_1 - ra_2 x_{t-1} + v_t$$

$$y_t = a_1(1-r) + a_2 x_t + ry_{t-1} - a_2 r x_{t-1} + v_t$$

$$y_t - ry_{t-1} = a_1(1-r) + a_2 x_t - rx_{t-1} + v_t.$$

Hence, we can estimate the following model:

$$y_t^* = a_1 x_{1t}^* + a_2 x_{2t}^* + v_t, \tag{5.8}$$

where $y_t^* = y_t - ry_{t-1}$, $x_{1t}^* = 1 - r$, $x_{2t}^* = x_t - rx_{t-1}$.

Prof. Metric reminds us to use the "Constant is Zero" or "No Constant" command in any econometric package, because x_{1t}^* is no longer a constant. Estimating model (5.8) will yield BLUE results because the serially correlated error, e_t, is substituted out. In practice, r is nonexistent, and we need the estimated autocorrelation coefficient of the errors $\hat{r}_k$ in equation (5.6).

He also reminds us that the predicted values are for $y_t^* = y_t - ry_{t-1}$, so we need to calculate the predicted value of y:

$$\hat{y}_t = \hat{y}_t^* + \hat{r}y_{t-1},$$

where y_{t-1} is the actual value of y at period $(t - 1)$, and $\hat{r}$ can be calculated using the formula in equation (5.6).

Autoregressive Models

We now move to the autoregressive (AR) model, which contains the lag dependent variables instead of the lag values of the error term. Prof. Metric says that this model requires special time-series analyses, because it involves only the dependent variable and its own lags instead of the addition of any external explanatory variable.

The Model

A dependent variable in an AR model can contain many lag values. Hence, the model can be denoted as AR(n) where n is the number of lag dependent variables, and the model is called the AR of order n. A model is called an autoregressive model of order one if the dependent variable is correlated to its first lag only. This model is denoted as AR(1) and can be written as:

$$y_t = ay_{t-1} + e_t. \tag{5.9}$$

If the coefficient estimate $|a| < 1$, then the series gradually approaches zero when the time, t, approaches infinity, and is said to be stationary. When $|a| \geq 1$, the series is said to be nonstationary. If $|a| > 1$, then the series explodes as t approaches infinity. If $|a| = 1$, then the series keeps winding aimlessly upward and downward with no real pattern and so is said to follow a random walk. In this case, equation (5.9) becomes:

$$y_t = y_{t-1} + e_t. \tag{5.10}$$

The model in equation (5.10) is called a "random walk," because the movement of the series is so random that the best you can guess about what happens in the next period is to look at the result in the current period and then add some random error to it. This behavior is in fact illustrated in equation (5.10).

Prof. Metric says that e_t is still assumed to be an independent random variable with a mean of zero and a constant variance. He also says that if all lag variables are stationary as in equation (5.9) and there is no autocorrelation, then the OLS estimation produces BLUE results. For example, a model with one constant and two lag values can be estimated using the OLS technique and is written as:

$$\hat{y}_t = \hat{a}_0 + \hat{a}_1 y_{t-1} + \hat{a}_2 y_{t-2}.$$

Point Prediction

Booka offers an example from her company: estimating a stationary AR(1) model of the demand for econometrics books gives the following results:

$$DEMAND_t = 69 + 0.9 \; DEMAND_{t-1}.$$

Demand value for last year is $DEMAND_{t-1} = 480$ volumes. Thus, we calculate the demand for this year as:

$$DEMAND_t = 69 + 0.9*480 = 501 \text{ (volumes)}.$$

This process can be extended into the future and is called "recursion by the law of iterated projections" (the recursive principle for short). The proof is provided in Hamilton (1994).

Interval Prediction

The formula for the standard error of the prediction $se(p)$ with T as the sample size is shown in Hill, Griffiths, and Lim (2011) as:

$$se\left(p\right)_{t+1} = s = \sqrt{\frac{SSE}{T - K}}. \tag{5.11}$$

Prof. Metric gives us an example of SSE = 120 and $T = 32$. He tells us to use these hypothetical values in calculating the interval prediction for this year.

We start with the point prediction of 501. The standard error of the prediction is:

$$s^2 = \frac{120}{32-2} = 4; \quad se(p)_{t+1} = s = \sqrt{4} = 2.$$

Next, we decide to choose a 95 percent confidence interval. Typing =TINV(0.05, 30) into an Excel cell gives us $t_C = t_{(0.975, 30)} = 2.042$. Finally, we calculate the interval prediction as:

$$DEMAND_t = 501 \pm 2*2.042 = (497; 505).$$

Thus, this year Booka will need to order between 497 and 505 volumes of econometrics books. We think it might be best to play it safe and follow the upper bound of 505 volumes.

First-Difference Model

Prof. Metric tells us that if a series follows a random walk, we might end up with a spurious regression, which produces significant regression results, but from completely unrelated data. There are two cases that need to be addressed separately. The first case is addressed in this section because it involves only lag dependent variables. The second case will be discussed in section 3 because it involves external lag variables.

If one of the lag dependent variables is unit coefficient ($a_k = 1$), then taking the first difference of the equation can turn it into a stationary series of a first-difference model. For example, taking the first difference of equation (5.10) yields the following model:

$$\Delta y_t = y_t - y_{t-1} = e_t. \tag{5.12}$$

Δy_t is a stationary series because e_t is an independent random variable with a mean of zero and a constant variance; there is no aimless factor in it. Any series that can be made stationary by taking the first difference (e.g., y_t in equation (5.10)) is said to be integrated of order one, which is denoted as an I(1) with the letter I standing for "integrated." The stationary model obtained by taking the first difference (e.g., Δy_t in equation (5.12)) is said to be integrated of order zero and is denoted as an $I(0)$.

This characteristic can be extended to estimating an $AR(n)$ model, in which $(n-1)$ series are stationary—for example, an $AR(2)$ model that has the first lag series nonstationary:

$$y_t = y_{t-1} + a_2 y_{t-2} + e_t, \text{ where } |a_2| < 1. \tag{5.13}$$

We can take the first difference of y_t to obtain the following model:

$$\Delta y_t = y_t - y_{t-1} = a_2 y_{t-2} + e_t. \tag{5.14}$$

Since the series becomes stationary, this equation can be estimated using the OLS technique.

We then have hands-on experience with an $I(0)$ model. Touro offers an equation for the values of his tour-package sales:

$$\Delta SALE_t = SALE_t - SALE_{t-1} = 0.11 * SALE_{t-2}.$$

Data on sale values for the previous years are: $SALE_{t-1}$ = \$4,400 and $SALE_{t-2}$ = \$4,600.

$$\Delta SALE_t = 0.11 * 4,600 = \$506.$$

We work on the problem and are able to calculate the predicted sale value for this year as:

$$SALE_t = \Delta SALE_t + SALE_{t-1} = \$506 + \$4,400 = \$4,906.$$

Prof. Metric tells us that an $I(1)$ series is also called a first-difference stationary series.

Other Simple Dynamic Models

We learn that this section only discusses other dynamic models under the assumption that all series are stationary. More in-depth discussions of nonstationarity will be offered in the later chapters.

Distributed Lag Models

Distributed lag (DL) models contain lag values of explanatory variables in addition to the lag dependent variables. If all classic assumptions are satisfied, then OLS can be performed.

A general DL model is written as:

$$y_t = a_0 + b_0 x_t + b_1 x_{t-1} + b_2 x_{t-2} + \ldots + b_k x_{t-k} + e_t. \qquad (5.15)$$

For example, if spending on nondurable goods (SPEND) depends on wage (WAGE) of current period and the past period, then the model is:

$$SPEND_t = 30 + 0.3 * WAGE_t + 0.2 * WAGE_{t-1}.$$

Suppose monthly data for $WAGE_t$ = \$2,800 and $WAGE_{t-1}$ = \$3,000, then the predicted value can be calculated as:

$$SPEND_t = 30 + 0.3 * 2,800 + 0.2 * 3,000 = 30 + 840 + 600 = 1,470$$

Interval prediction can be calculated using the formula for the standard error of the prediction in equation (5.11).

Autoregressive Distributed Lag Models

Another model, which includes lagged dependent variables in addition to other explanatory variables, is called the autoregressive distributed lag (ARDL) model. Again, if all classic assumptions are observed, then OLS can be performed. For example:

$$SPEND_t = 60 + 0.4 * SPEND_{t-1} + 0.4 * WAGE_{t-1}. \qquad (5.16)$$

Suppose $WAGE_{t-1}$ = \$3,000 and $SPEND_{t-1}$ = \$2,000 for previous month, then a prediction can be obtained:

$$SPEND_t = 60 + 0.4 * 3000 + 0.4 * 2000 = 60 + 1,200 + 800 = 2,060.$$

We learn that a general ARDL should have lagged values of the dependent variables in addition to current and lagged values of the other explanatory variables. The model is written as follows:

$$y_t = a_0 + a_1 y_{t-1} + a_2 y_{t-2} + \ldots + a_p y_{t-p} + b_0 x_1 + b_1 x_{t-1} +$$

$$b_2 x_{t-2} + \ldots + b_q x_{t-q} + e_t. \tag{5.17}$$

That is, if we use the notation ARDL(p, q) for the model, then p represents the number of lagged y's, and q represents the number of lagged x's. For example, an ARDL(1, 2) is called an ARDL of order (1,2) and is written as:

$$y_t = a_0 + a_1 y_{t-1} + b_0 x_t + b_1 x_{t-1} + b_2 x_{t-2} + e_t. \tag{5.18}$$

In this case, we will lose two data points when we generate the data for our regressions (in fact, we only lose one observation for y but two observations for x, so we still have to eliminate the first two rows in the dataset). Note that we also lose five degrees of freedom performing any hypothetical test on the model in equation (5.18).

To decide how many lag values we should include in an ARDL model, we should make sure that there is no omitted variable by checking on the statistical significance of coefficient estimates. Other than that, we should use fewest numbers of lags that eliminates serial correlation. Including too many lag values will increase the number of irrelevant variables and inflate the variances of coefficient estimates.

Data Analyses

Prof. Empirie tells us that we will apply Excel estimation to most of the models learned in the theoretical sections: models with lag values of the error (autocorrelation), models with lag dependent variables (AR models), those with lag values of the explanatory variables (DL models), and unit root test for all three models. However, Excel is not the ideal software to perform a Box-Jenkins procedure, so we will skip this procedure.

Autocorrelation

Testing Autocorrelation

The file *Ch05.xls., Fig 5.1* contains data on salary (SAL) and spending (SPEND). We notice that Prof. Empirie has also copied and pasted SAL in column A into column E for our convenience in a later regression. First, we regress SPEND on SAL:

> Click on Data and then Data Analysis on the ribbon.
> Select Regression, then click OK.
> Enter B1:B34 in the Input Y Range box.
> Enter A1:A34 in the Input X Range box.
> Choose Labels and Residuals.
> Check the Output Range button and enter G1.
> Click OK then OK again to override the data range.
> Copy and paste the residuals (e_t) into column C.
> Generate e_{t-1} by copying and pasting cells C2 through C34 into cells D3 through D35.
> Copy and paste SAL in column A into column E (here the action has already been done by Prof. Empirie).

Next, we regress the Residuals e_t on e_{t-1} and SAL.

> Click Data and then Data Analysis on the ribbon.
> Select Regression, then click OK.
> For Input Y Range: enter B3:B34.
> For Input X Range: enter D3:E34.
> Uncheck the box Labels—that is, do not use Labels.
> Check the Output Range button and enter Q1.
> Click OK and then OK again to override the data range.

Figure 5.1 shows sections of this second regression with the number of observations and R^2.

From this figure, $T = 32$ and $R^2 = 0.79$, so $LM_{STAT} = 32*0.79 = 25.28$. Typing =*CHIINV(0.05,1)* into any cell gives you $\chi^2_{(1)} = 3.84$. Since $LM_{STAT} > \chi^2_c$, we reject the null hypothesis, meaning r is different from zero and implying that autocorrelation exists.

	SUMMARY OUTPUT				
	Regression Statistics				
	Multiple R	0.888813573			
	R Square	0.789989567			
	Adjusted R Square	0.775506089			
	Standard Error	341.5545249			
	Observations	32			
	ANOVA				
		df	*SS*	*MS*	*F*	*Significance F*
	Regression	2	12726194.93	6363097.464	54.54418903	1.48762E-10
	Residual	29	3383125.311	116659.4935		
	Total	31	16109320.24			

Figure 5.1 T and R^2 for autocorrelation test

Prof. Empirie points out to us that we always use R^2 instead of adjusted R^2 even when the model has more than one explanatory variable. This is also true for the heteroscedasticity tests in Chapter 4 because we wish to play safe and avoid missing the borderline cases.

Regressing with Autocorrelation

Prof. Empirie tells us that the first four columns of the file *Ch05.xls. Fig.5.2* are the same as those in the file *Ch05.xls.Fig.5.1*. The commands for this section will continue from that step.

In cell E3 type =C3^2, then press Enter.
Copy and paste the formula into cells E4 through E34.
In cell F3 type =C3*D3, then press Enter.
Copy and paste the formula into cells F4 through F34.
In cell E35 type =SUM(E3:E34), then press Enter.
Copy and paste the formula into cells F35.
In cell G3 type =F35/E35, then press Enter.
Copy and Paste Special the value in cell G3 into cells G4 through G34.
Copy and paste the values in cells B2 through B34 into cells H3 through H35.
Copy and paste the values in cells A2 through A34 into cells I3 through I35.
In cell J3 type =B3 – (G3*H3), then press Enter (this is SPEND*).
Copy and paste the formula into cells J4 through J34.

In cell K3 type $= 1 - G3$, then press Enter (this is X1*).
Copy and paste the formula into cells K4 through K34.
In cell L3 type $= A3 - (G3*I3)$, then press Enter (this is SAL*).
Copy and paste the formula into cells L4 through L34.

Next, we need to regress SPEND* on X1* and SAL*.

Go to Data Analysis and choose Regression, then click OK.
In the Input Y Range box enter J2:J34.
In the Input X Range box enter K2:L34.
Check the box Labels, Constant is Zero, and Residuals.
Check the Output Range button and enter P1.
Click OK then OK again to obtain the results.

Figure 5.2 reports the regression results.
From this figure, the estimated equation is:

$$\text{SPEND*}_t = 3015.65 \ X1^*_{t-1} + 0.0009 \ \text{SAL*}_{t-1};$$
$$(\text{se}) \qquad (170.355) \qquad (0.00271)$$
$$\text{Adjusted } R^2 = 0.9087; \qquad T = 32.$$

Because $SPEND^* = SPEND_t - rSPEND_{t-1}$, to obtain predicted values of $SPEND_t$:

Copy and paste the values in cells Q26 through Q57 into cells M3
    through M34.
In cell N3 type $= M3 + G3*H3$, then press Enter.
Copy and paste the formula into cells N4 through N34.

	O	P	Q	R	S	T	U	V	W	X	Y
4		Multiple R	0.97156								
5		R Square	0.94392								
6		Adjusted R Square	0.90872								
7		Standard Error	209.854								
8		Observations	32								
9											
10		ANOVA									
11			df	SS	MS	F	gnificance F				
12		Regression	2	2.2E+07	1.1E+07	252.494	4.5E-19				
13		Residual	30	1321167	44038.9						
14		Total	32	2.4E+07							
15											
16			Coefficient	andard Err	t Stat	P-value	lower 95%	Jpper 95%	ower 95.0%	pper 95.0%	
17		Intercept	0	#N/A	#N/A	#N/A	#N/A	#N/A	#N/A	#N/A	
18		X1*	3015.65	170.355	17.7022	2E-17	2667.73	3363.56	2667.73	3363.56	
19		SAL*	0.0009	0.00271	0.33082	0.74308	-0.0046	0.00644	-0.0046	0.00644	

Figure 5.2 Regressing with autocorrelation: The results

We learn that we can calculate interval prediction as usual.

DL Models

Invo has collected data on the Singapore-Australia real exchange rate (EXCHA) and exports from Australia to Singapore (EXPS) in millions of dollars. The data are available in the file *Ch05.xls.Fig. 5.3.* We proceed to regress $EXPS_t$ on $EXCHA_{t-1}$:

> Click on Data and then Data Analysis on the ribbon.
> Select Regression in the list, then click OK.
> A dialog box appears.
> Enter B1:B33 n the Input Y Range box.
> Enter C1:C33 in the Input X Range box.
> Choose Labels and Residuals.
> Check the Output Range button and enter E1.
> Click OK then OK again to overwrite the data.

The results of the estimated coefficients are displayed in Figure 5.3.

In the data file, the predicted value of $EXPS_{2013}$ is in cell F56. The value can be verified by this equation:

$$EXPS_{2013} = -9929.6148 + 4807.4210 \ EXCHA_{2012}$$
$$= -9929.6148 + 4807.4210* \ 6.98 \approx 23,626 \ \text{(in millions of dollars)}.$$

SUMMARY OUTPUT						
Regression Statistics						
Multiple R	0.374690088					
R Square	0.140392662					
Adjusted R Square	0.111739084					
Standard Error	22651.0473					
Observations	32					
ANOVA						
	df	*SS*	*MS*	*F*	*gnificance F*	
Regression	1	2513866001	2.51E+09	4.899656	0.034609	
Residual	30	15392098311	5.13E+08			
Total	31	17905964312				
	Coefficients	*Standard Error*	*t Stat*	*P-value*	*Lower 95%*	*Upper 95%* *Lower 95.0%* *Upper 95.0%*
Intercept	-9929.614766	15531.36747	-0.63933	0.527463	-41648.9 21789.67	-41648.9 21789.67
EXCHAt-1	4807.421043	2171.847788	2.213517	0.034609	371.9161 9242.926	371.9161 9242.926

Figure 5.3 DL model: Regression results

Prof. Empirie says that the estimation procedure for an ARDL model is a combination of an AR model estimation and a DL estimation; thus, there is no need to discuss in detail in the class.

Exercises

1. The file Energy.xls contains data on energy demand in Hawaii. Estimate the AR(1) model by regressing energy period t on energy period $t-1$.
2. Obtain the interval prediction using the results in Question 1 and a handheld calculator.
3. Given the information in Table 5.1, use a hand calculator to compute the sample correlation of $\hat{e}_t$ with $\hat{e}_{t-1}$ and $\hat{e}_{t-2}$, then make a decision on the autocorrelation problem.

Table 5.1 Residuals from an OLS estimation with sample size T = 4

t	1	2	3	4
$\hat{e}_t$	−0.18	0.4	−0.34	0.045

CHAPTER 6

Panel Data Techniques

Taila asks, "Prof. Empirie introduced us to longitudinal/panel datasets in chapter 2, but we have not discussed anything on using them. I was wondering if you could provide us with more information." Prof. Metric responds enthusiastically that we will learn panel data analysis this week. He says that upon finishing this chapter, we will be able to:

1. Explain the nature and advantages of learning panel data techniques;
2. Master panel data techniques in obtaining regression coefficients;
3. Discuss the goodness-of-fit issue that arises with the panel data technique;
4. Use Excel to carry out corresponding analyses.

Nature of Panel Data

Prof. Metric reminds the class that a panel dataset combines a cross-sectional dataset with a time-series dataset. Invo asks, "Why does one have to learn panel data techniques?" Taila volunteers to give an example of the advantage of using panel data. If we have a time-series dataset on pajama sales in Korea for 15 months and another dataset on pajama sales in China for the same 15 months, then combining the two datasets gives us a sample size of 30 data points.

Prof. Metric praises Taila on offering a good example and says that another advantage of using the panel data technique is that we will be able to observe more than one identity over time to control for the individual heterogeneity. In this particular case, the observation provides us with additional information on the specific characteristics of each market. For example, we can understand demand for pajamas in Northeast Asia by studying pajama sales in Korea and China. In addition, we are able to carry out a comparative study over a period of time. For example, we can compare demand in Korea over the past five years with demand in China during the same time period and then develop different strategies to increase sales in each country.

Panel data can be divided into "short-and-wide" panels or "long-and-narrow" panels. If I is the number of individuals observed in each of T time periods, then a short-and-wide panel has $I > T$ while a long-and-narrow panel has $T > I$. Panel data can also be divided into balanced and unbalanced panels, with the unbalanced panels having some observations missing, while the balanced ones do not have any missing observation. Prof. Metric says that Excel cannot handle missing observations, so we need to delete the whole row if we run into this problem.

We learn that we can use OLS to run regression on a panel dataset if the two identities have the same characteristics; for example, if pajama sales in Korea and China have the same pattern, then the coefficient estimates will be the same for the two countries. If this is the case, all we have to do is stack one dataset above the other and then run a regression called a "pooled OLS" estimation to extend the dataset to 30 data points, as mentioned by Taila, so that CLT will guarantee valid test results. Hence, the model for the pooled OLS is:

$$y_{it} = a_1 + a_2 x_{2it} + a_3 x_{3it} + e_{it}. \tag{6.1}$$

Prof. Metric reminds us to notice that the parameters a_1, a_2, and a_3, are still the same as those in Chapter 3, even though each of the variables and the error term have the subscript "it" added.

$$a_{1it} = a_1; \quad a_{2it} = a_2; \quad a_{3it} = a_3.$$

We understand that all the classic assumptions have to hold for us to use this pooled OLS estimator, specifically,

$$E(e_{it}) = 0; \ \text{var} \ (e_{it}) = E(e_{2it}) = \sigma^2,$$
$$Cov(e_{it}, e_{iz}) = E(e_{it}, e_{iz}) = 0 \ \text{for} \ i \neq j \ \text{or} \ t \neq z,$$
$$Cov(e_{it}, x_{2it}) = Cov(e_{it}, x_{3it}) = 0. \tag{6.2}$$

We all feel that the two markets cannot have the exact same characteristics most of the time. Prof. Metric says that in this case, stacking two or more datasets for different identities will bias the coefficient estimates, and the variances will be inflated, so the tests will be invalid. He tells us that the most general case of panel data is written as:

$$y_{it} = a_{1it} + a_{2it}x_{2it} + a_{3it}x_{3it} + e_{it}. \tag{6.3}$$

Booka exclaims, "Oh… I now see that each of the parameters a_{1it}, a_{2it}, and a_{3it} has the subscript *it*." Prof. Metric, says, "Yes, this model allows for each identity to be different across sections and over time." He continues by stating that we cannot estimate this model because there are not enough data points to cover all the unknown parameters. Hence, some simplifications are needed. The first way is to allow the identities to be different in their intercepts:

$$y_{it} = a_{1i} + a_2 x_{2it} + a_3 x_{3it} + e_{it}. \tag{6.4}$$

Prof. Metric reminds us to note the subscript *i* as in a_{1i}, which indicates different intercepts across the identities; whereas, the variables a_2 and a_3 do not have this subscript, implying that the identities have the same slope. The model in equation (6.4) assumes that all behavioral differences among the identities are captured by the constant term, so that:

$$a_{1it} = a_{1i}; \quad a_{2it} = a_2; \quad a_{3it} = a_3.$$

Another case occurs when sectional individuals have different slopes:

$$y_{it} = a_1 + a_{2i}x_{2it} + a_{3i}x_{3it} + e_{it}. \tag{6.5}$$

The third case combines equations (6.4) and (6.5):

$$y_{it} = a_{1i} + a_{2i}x_{2it} + a_{3i}x_{3it} + e_{it}. \tag{6.6}$$

These differences in characteristics are unobserved effects that need to be removed. Panel data techniques can be applied for either case, and more cases will be discussed later.

Panel Data Techniques

We first focus on the model in equation (6.4) using either the first-difference estimation or the fixed-effects estimation.

First-Difference Estimation

Given the model in equation (6.4), we can add a second equation by retrogressing one period:

$$y_{it} = a_{1i} + a_2 x_{2it} + a_3 x_{3it} + e_{it};$$

$$y_{i,t-1} = a_{1i} + a_2 x_{2i,t-1} + a_3 x_{3i,t-1} + e_{i,t-1}.$$

Subtract the second equation from the first:

$$y_{it} - y_{i,t-1} = a_2 \left(x_{2it} - x_{2i,t-1} \right) + a_3 \left(x_{3it} - x_{3i,t-1} \right) + \left(e_{it} - e_{i,t-1} \right)$$

$$\Delta y_{it} = a_2 \Delta x_{2it} + a_3 \Delta x_{3it} + \Delta e_{it}. \tag{6.7}$$

The model in equation (6.7) will control for the difference in the intercepts because the constant term in equation (6.4) has been eliminated and no longer exists in equation (6.7).

Prof. Metric then tells us that the suitable case for using a first-difference model, instead of the fixed-effects model, is when the error term follows a random walk (Wooldridge 2013).

$$y_{it} = a_{1i} + a_2 x_{2it} + a_3 x_{3it} + e_{it},$$

where $e_{it} = e_{i,t-1} + v_{it}$,
where v_t satisfies all the classic assumptions:

$$E(v_{it}) = 0; \ \text{var}\,(v_{it}) = E(v_{2it}) = s^2;$$
$$\text{Cov}(v_{it}, v_{jz}) = E(v_{it}, v_{jz}) = 0 \text{ for } i \neq j \text{ or } t \neq z;$$
$$\text{Cov}(v_{it}, x_{2it}) = \text{Cov}(v_{it}, x_{3it}) = 0.$$

Taking the first difference yields:

$$y_{it} - y_{i,t-1} = a_2 \left(x_{2it} - x_{2i,t-1} \right) + a_3 \left(x_{3it} - x_{3i,t-1} \right) + \left(e_{it} - e_{i,t-1} \right).$$

In this case, taking the first difference serves two purposes: (*i*) elimination of the intercept a_{1i} presented in equation (6.4) and (*ii*) correcting for the autocorrelation of the errors. Since v_t satisfies all the classic assumptions, there is no longer an autocorrelation problem.

An example of the first-difference estimation is the following model:

$$HOUSE_{it} = a_{1i} + a_2 INCOME_{it} + a_3 CREDIT_{it} + e_{it}; e_t = e_{t-1} + v_t,$$

where *HOUSE* is the average value of investment in residential housing, *INCOME* is per capita income, and *CREDIT* is the investment credit from the federal government. Going backward one period and subtracting the second equation from the first yields:

$$\Delta HOUSE_{it} = a_2 \Delta INCOME_{it} + a_3 \Delta CREDIT_{it} + \Delta e_{it}.$$

Suppose that the regression results are:

$$\Delta HOUSE_{it} = 1.2\ \Delta INCOME_{it} + 0.3\ \Delta CREDIT_{it},$$

where $\Delta INCOME_{it}$ = \$8,000 and $\Delta CREDIT_{it}$ = \$ 5,000, then the point prediction of the investment in housing is:

$$\Delta HOUSE_{it} = 1.2 * 4,000 + 0.3 * 5,000 = 9,600 + 1,500 = \$11,100.$$

Since this is a change in the investment value instead of the investment value itself, we can calculate the predicted value of the investment as follows:

$$\Delta HOUSE_{it} = HOUSE_{it} - HOUSE_{i,t-1},$$

$$HOUSE_{it} = \Delta HOUSE_{it} + HOUSE_{i,t-1}.$$

Suppose data on the previous period provides the average investment value as $HOUSE_{i,t-1}$ = \$150,000, then the predicted value is:

$$HOUSE_{it} = \$11,100 + \$150,000 = \$161,100.$$

We learn that the concept of differencing can be extended to more than two periods. For example, a three-period difference model will be as follows:

$$\Delta y_{i,t} = a_2 \Delta x_{2i,t} + a_3 \Delta x_{3i,t} + a_4 \Delta x_{3i,t-1} + \Delta e_{i,t} + \Delta e_{i,t-1}.$$

Prof. Metric tells us that in this case, a comma is often placed between the subscript for the identity and the time period to avoid any confusion on the meaning of the notation.

Fixed-Effects Estimation

Next, Prof. Metric shows us another method of controlling for the differences in the intercepts by using the "fixed effects" estimation. We again zero in on the difference in intercepts first. The theoretical model is obtained by taking the deviation from the mean, so we have to take the time average values of equation (6.4):

$$\bar{y}_{it} = a_{1i} + a_2 \bar{x}_{2it} + a_3 \bar{x}_{3it} + \bar{e}_{it}. \tag{6.8}$$

We then subtract equation (6.8) from equation (6.4):

$$y_{it} - \bar{y}_{it} = a_2 \left(x_{2it} - \bar{x}_{2it} \right) + a_3 \left(x_{3it} - \bar{x}_{3it} \right) + \left(e_{it} - \bar{e}_{it} \right).$$

We now can perform forecasts on the following model using OLS:

$$\tilde{y}_{it} = a_2 \tilde{x}_{2it} + a_3 \tilde{x}_{3it} + \tilde{e}_{it}, \tag{6.9}$$

where

$$\tilde{y}_{it} = y_{it} - \bar{y}_{it}; \ \tilde{x}_{2it} = (x_{2it} - \bar{x}_{2it}); \ \tilde{x}_{3it} = (x_{3it} - \bar{x}_{3it}); \ \tilde{e}_{it} = (e_{it} - \bar{e}_{it}).$$

The transformed model in (6.9) will control the fixed effects problem because the intercept term in equation (6.4) has been removed from equation (6.9). The data are said to be "demeaned" because we take the deviation from the mean of the data.

In practice, the most convenient and flexible way to carry out regression on a fixed-effects model is to use the least square dummy variable (LSDV) method whenever the number of identities is not too large (less than 100 identities or time periods). To obtain the LSDV estimators for equation (6.4), we generate a dummy variable for each of the identities. Suppose we have six different identities, then:

$$D_{1i} = \begin{cases} 1 & i = 1 \\ 0 & \text{otherwise} \end{cases}, \quad D_{2i} = \begin{cases} 1 & i = 2 \\ 0 & \text{otherwise} \end{cases}, \dots, \quad D_{6i} = \begin{cases} 1 & i = 6 \\ 0 & \text{otherwise} \end{cases}.$$

With these six dummies added, equation (6.4) can be written as:

$$y_{it} = a_{11}D_{1i} + a_{12}D_{2i} + \dots + a_{16}D_{6i} + a_2 x_{2it} + a_3 x_{3it} + e_{it}. \quad (6.10)$$

Prof. Metric reminds us to suppress the constant, because the model (eq. 6.9) no longer has a constant.

Prof. Metric continues with the example of pajama sales in Korea and China and gives us this model:

$$SALE_{it} = a_{1i} + a_2 PRICE_{it} + a_3 PROM_{it} + e_{it},$$

where SALE is the values of pajama sales, PRICE is price of pajamas, and PROM is the expenditures on sale promotion. He asks us to write a model to control for the difference in sale characteristics in the two countries.

We decide to use the LSDV model and see that only the intercept term is different between the two countries, as indicated by the subscript i, so we add two intercept dummies: D_K = Korea and D_C = China and write the model as:

$$SALE_{it} = a_{11}D_K + a_{12}D_C + a_2 PRICE_{it} + a_3 PROM_{it} + e_{it},$$

where $D_K = \begin{cases} 1 & i = \text{Korea} \\ 0 & \text{otherwise} \end{cases}$ and $D_C = \begin{cases} 1 & i = \text{China} \\ 0 & \text{otherwise} \end{cases}.$

We also tell Prof. Metric that we will have to suppress the constant when running the regression, and he is very pleased that we remembered the details of this method.

Touro then asks, "We learned in chapter 4 that a researcher can only add (G–1) dummies. Why do we have to use two dummies for two groups here?" Prof. Metric commends Touro on the question and says that we already suppressed the constant, so there is no perfect collinearity here, and the reason we want to add two dummies is that we want to control for different characteristics in both countries.

He then says that if the two markets also differ over time, then adding time dummies to the equation will help:

$$SALE_{it} = a_{11}D_K + a_{12}D_C + a_2 PRICE_{it} + a_3 PROM_{it} + b_1 t_1 + \ldots + b_T t_T + e_{it}$$

Invo asks, "Can we add the slopes in addition to the time dummies? Or had we better stick to the model in (6.6)?" Prof. Metric says, "We can add the slope dummies to the equation, so using either cross-sectional or a combination of cross-sectional and time dummies is fine." Combining the two produces this model:

$$\begin{aligned} SALE_{it} = {}& a_{11}D_K + a_{12}D_C + a_2 PRICE_{it} + a_3 PROM_{it} + b_1 t_1 + \ldots + b_T t_T \\ & + c_1 \left(D_K * PRICE_{it} \right) + c_2 \left(D_C * PRICE_{it} \right) + d_1 \left(D_K * PROM_{it} \right) \\ & + d_2 \left(D_C * PROM_{it} \right) + e_{it} \end{aligned}$$

Prof. Metric also tells us that we will learn more applications of time dummies and slope dummies in later chapters.

Seemingly Unrelated Regressions (SUR)

Because this method requires econometric software packages other than Excel, Prof. Metric only provides us with a quick introduction. Suppose that we have three equations for Singapore (1), Myanmar (2), and Laos (3). SUR estimations assume that the errors of these three equations exhibit contemporaneous correlation in the same period. The basic SUR estimation, which is a GLS procedure, can be performed in three steps, as follows:

(i) Estimate the three equations separately using OLS.
(ii) Use the residuals from the OLS estimation in step (i) to estimate the variances $\sigma_{(1)}^2, \sigma_{(2)}^2, \sigma_{(3)}^2$, and the covariance $\sigma_{(1),(2),(3)}^2$.

(iii) Use the estimates from step (*ii*) to regress the three equations jointly within a GLS framework.

This method is usually very effective for identities of the same region (Southeast Asia in this case), country, state, or city, because they are often correlated with each other.

Detecting Different Characteristics

Since pooled OLS can be performed when all identities or time periods have the same characteristics, we need to perform a test on these characteristics. For example, we want to know if the equations for Korea and China have identical parameters. This is an *F*-test, called the Chow test, for the significance of the dummy variable. The restricted model is:

$$SALE_{it} = a_{11} + a_2 PRICE_{it} + a_3 PROM_{it} + e_{it}.$$

For the purpose of testing the preceding equation, the unrestricted model needs only one dummy added because a_{11} already catches characteristics of one of the two countries, those of Korea in this case, so the equation is:

$$SALE_{it} = a_{11} + a_{12} D_C + a_2 PRICE_{it} + a_3 PROM_{it} + e_{it}.$$

Suppose $a_{12} = 0$, then China shares the same characteristics with Korea, so the hypotheses are written as:

$$H_0 : a_{12} = 0; \ H_a : a_{12} \neq 0.$$

Assuming that heteroscedasticity or serial correlation is not a problem with this model, the formula for *F*-statistics is similar to the one discussed in chapters 3 and 4, with the same definitions for *J* and *K*, except that we have a panel data, so:

$$F_{STAT} = \frac{(SSE_R - SSE_U)/J}{SSE_U/(IT - K)} \text{ and } F_c = F_{(J, IT-K)}, \qquad (6.11)$$

where *IT* is the sample size with *I* = the number of observations across identities and *T* = the number of observations over time.

Prof. Metric reminds us that we still have to perform the test in the four standard steps. If the *F*-statistic is greater than *F*-critical, then we reject H_0, and the two equations do not have identical coefficients, so a panel-data technique is needed for estimations.

Goodness-of-Fit

Prof. Metric tells us that eliminating the constant amounts to regressing through the origin. This procedure causes the R^2 value to become an unreliable measure for the goodness-of-fit, which is also compromised for several other models in Volume Two. For this reason, he introduces the Root Mean Squared Error (RMSE) here so that we know an alternative measure for the goodness-of-fit:

$$RMSE = \sqrt{\frac{\sum\limits_{i=1}^{I} (y_i - \hat{y}_i)^2}{I}} = \sqrt{\frac{\sum\limits_{i=1}^{I} \hat{e}_i^2}{I}}. \qquad (6.12)$$

We then work on an RMSE example given the information in Table 6.1.

We then calculate the mean squared errors (MSE):

$$MSE = (1 + 2 + 4)/3 = 2.33.$$

Finally, we take the square root of the MSE:

$$RMSE = \sqrt{2.33} = 1.53.$$

Prof. Metric says that the smaller the RMSE, the better fit a model is.

Table 6.1 Steps for calculating RMSE

(1)	(2)	(3)	(4)	(5)
Observation	y	$\hat{y}$	$y - \hat{y}$	$(y - \hat{y})^2$
1	8	7	8 − 7 = 1	$1^2 = 1$
2	9	8	9 − 8 = 1	$1^2 = 2$
3	7	9	7 − 9 = − 2	$(- 2)^2 = 4$

Data Analyses

Taila shares with us a yearly dataset on output per worker (OUT) and exports (EXPS) for Malaysia, Australia, and Cambodia during the years 2007 to 2015. She has downloaded the data from the World Bank website. Since one lagged variable is generated, we have data for the years 2008 to 2015 to perform the regressions and tests. We find that the data are in the file *Ch06.xls, Fig. 6.1.*

Testing Different Characteristics

The restricted model is:

$$EXPS_{it} = a_{11} + a_2 OUT_{i,t-1} + e_{it}.$$

The unrestricted model is:

$$EXPS_{it} = a_{11} + a_{1A} D_A + a_{1C} D_C + OUT_{i,t-1} + e_{it}. \qquad (6.13)$$

D_A and D_C are the dummies for Australia and Cambodia, respectively. Prof. Empirie reminds us that the three countries will share the same characteristics if $a_{1A} = a_{1C} = 0$, so we only need two dummies for the test.

To perform the cross-equation test on the three countries, we first estimate the restricted model by regressing EXPS on OUT:

Go to Data then Data Analysis.
Select Regression, then click OK.
The input Y range is E1:E25, the input X range is G1:G25.
Check the box Labels.
Check the button Output Range and enter L1.
Click OK then OK again to overwrite the data.

Next, we regress EXPS on OUT, D_A and D_C:

Go to Data then Data Analysis.
Select Regression, then click OK.
The input Y range is E1:E25, the input X range is G1:I25.

Check the box Labels.

Check the button Output Range and enter L20.

Click OK then OK again to overwrite the data.

The Analysis of Variance (ANOVA) sections that report the SSEs for the two models are displayed in Figure 6.1. We find that SEE_R is reported in cell X4 and SSE_U in cell AC4.

From the results in this figure, the four steps for the test are:

(i) $H_0: a_{1A} = a_{1C} = 0$; $H_a: a_{1A} \neq 0$, or $a_{1C} \neq 0$, or both $\neq 0$.

(ii) $F_{STAT} = \dfrac{\left(2.35 * 10^9 - 5.73 * 10^8\right)/2}{5.73 * 10^8 / (24 - 4)} = \dfrac{8.89}{0.2865} = 31.03.$

(iii) We decide to use $\alpha = 0.05$ and type = FINV (0.05, 2, 20) into an Excel cell, which gives us $F_C = 3.49$.

(iv) Since $F_{STAT} > F_C$, we reject the null, meaning at least one pair of parameters is different and implying that a panel-data estimation is needed.

Estimating with Panel Data

First-Difference Estimation

We find that the data are in the file *Ch06.xls, Fig. 6.2.* The model is

$$\Delta EXPS_{it} = \Delta OUT_{i,t-1} + e_{it}.$$

We have to perform the following steps:

	U	V	W	X	Y	Z	AA	AB	AC	AD	AE
1		ANOVA					ANOVA				
2			df	SS	MS			df	SS	MS	
3		Regression	1	12388086317	12388086317		Regression	3	14161997930	4720665977	
4		Residual	22	2347308270	106695830.4		Residual	20	573396656.8	28669832.84	
5		Total	23	14735394587			Total	23	14735394587		

Figure 6.1 ANOVA sections for restricted and unrestricted models, respectively

In cell H2 type =*D2 – E2*, then press Enter.

In cell I2 type =*F2 – G2*, then press Enter.

Copy cells H2 through I2 and paste into cells H3 through I25.

Go to Data then Data Analysis.

Select Regression, then click OK.

The input Y range is H1:H25, the input X range is I1:I25.

Check the boxes Labels; Constant is Zero.

Check the Residuals button to obtain the predicted values.

Check the button Output Range and enter K1.

Click OK then OK again to overwrite the data.

Figure 6.2 shows that the results for the intercept are suppressed and reported as #N/A.

Prof. Empirie points out that we were estimating the change of the variables, so we need to follow the theoretical equation to recover the intercept for predictions:

$$y_{it} = a_{1i} + a_2 x_{2it} + a_3 x_{3it},$$

so,

$$a_{1i} = y_{it} - \left(a_2 x_{2it} + a_3 x_{3it} \right). \tag{6.14}$$

	K	L	M	N	O	P	Q	R	S
1	SUMMARY OUTPUT								
2									
3	*Regression Statistics*								
4	Multiple R	0.14706667							
5	R Square	0.0216286							
6	Adjusted R Squar	-0.02184966							
7	Standard Error	5020.61159							
8	Observations	24							
9									
10	ANOVA								
11		*df*	*SS*	*MS*	*F*	*ignificance F*			
12	Regression	1	12816393.7	1.3E+07	0.50846	0.4933			
13	Residual	23	579730436	2.5E+07					
14	Total	24	592566830						
15									
16		*Coefficients*	*Standard Error*	*t Stat*	*P-value*	*Lower 95%*	*Upper 95%*	*ower 95.0%*	*Upper 95.0%*
17	Intercept	0	#N/A	#N/A	#N/A	#N/A	#N/A	#N/A	#N/A
18	ΔOUTt	0.22638395	0.31748217	0.71306	0.48298	-0.43038	0.88315	-0.43038	0.88315

Figure 6.2 Results for first-difference estimation

Once the intercept is recovered, we can substitute it into the estimated equation to calculate the point and interval predictions as usual.

Fixed-Effects Estimation

We find that the data are in the file *Ch06.xls, Fig. 6.3.* Prof. Empirie reminds us that theoretically, we can perform a fixed-effects model by using the demeaned model. Empirically, it is much more convenient to use the LSDV techniques, so we are going to perform an LSDV estimation, and the regression equation is:

$$EXPS_{it} = a_{1A}D_A + a_{1C}D_C + a_{1M}D_M + OUT_{i,t-1} + e_{it}.$$

We are sure that you noticed the three dummies added to the equation and that the constant is suppressed from this equation. You should perform the following regression steps:

Go to Data then Data Analysis.
Select Regression, then click OK.
The input Y range is E1:E25, the input X range is G1:J25.
Check the boxes Labels; Constant is Zero.
Check the Residuals button to obtain the predicted values.
Check the button Output Range and enter L1.
Click OK then OK again to overwrite the data.

The results are reported in Figure 6.3. You can see that we use all three dummies to control for the fixed effects.

Prof. Empirie reminds us that recovering the intercept is possible by using the model:

$$\bar{y}_{it} = a_{11} + a_2\bar{x}_{2it},$$

so,

$$a_{11} = \bar{y}_{it} - a_2\bar{x}_{2it}. \tag{6.15}$$

	K	L	M	N	O	P	Q	R	S	T	U
1		SUMMARY OUTPUT									
2											
3		*Regression Statistics*									
4		Multiple R	0.995330138								
5		R Square	0.990682084								
6		Adjusted R Square	0.939284397								
7		Standard Error	5354.421803								
8		Observations	24								
9											
10		ANOVA									
11			*df*	*SS*	*MS*	*F*	*gnificance F*				
12		Regression	4	60963612674	1.52E+10	531.6007	3.28E-19				
13		Residual	20	573396656.8	28669833						
14		Total	24	61537009331							
15											
16			*Coefficients*	*Standard Error*	*t Stat*	*P-value*	*Lower 95%*	*Upper 95%*	*ower 95.0%*	*ipper 95.0%*	
17		Intercept	0	#N/A	#N/A	#N/A	#N/A	#N/A	#N/A	#N/A	
18		OUTt-1	0.139969061	0.207046251	0.676028	0.506766	-0.29192	0.57186	-0.29192	0.57186	
19		DA	9516.020896	9001.731991	1.057132	0.303054	-9261.26	28293.3	-9261.26	28293.3	
20		DC	74415.7972	1994.50358	37.31044	5.76E-20	70255.34	78576.26	70255.34	78576.26	
21		DM	39211.87123	4771.820613	8.217382	7.68E-08	29258.03	49165.71	29258.03	49165.71	

Figure 6.3 Results for fixed-effects estimation

Once the intercept is recovered, substitute it into the estimated equation to calculate the point and interval predictions as usual.

Exercises

1. The file Growth.xls contains data on GDP growth (GROW), investment (INV), and money growth (MONEY) for four regions A, B, C, and D for 10 years. Assuming that the four regions differ in intercepts only,
   (a) Perform a regression of GROW on INV and MONEY using the first difference technique.
   (b) Report the results using the standard format learned in chapter 3.
2. Using the dataset from Exercise 1,
   (a) Perform a regression of GROW on INV and MONEY using the LSDV technique.
   (b) Provide an interpretation of MONEY, including magnitude and significance level.
3. Use the results in Exercise 2 to provide point and interval predictions for INV and MONEY.

Bibliography

Bartlett, M.S. 1946. "On the Theoretical Specification of Sampling Properties of Autocorrelated Time Series." *Journal of the Royal Statistical Society* 8, no. 27, pp. 24–32.

Davidson, R., and J. MacKinnon. 2004. *Econometric Theory and Method.* New York, NY: Oxford University Press.

Greene, W.H. 2012. *Econometric Analysis.* Upper Saddle River, NJ: Prentice Hall.

Hamilton, J.D. 1994. *Time Series Analysis.* Princeton, NJ: Princeton University Press.

Hill, R.C., W.E. Griffiths, and G.C. Lim. 2011. *Principle of Econometrics.* Hoboken, NJ: Wiley and Son.

IMF Data and Statistics Website. 2017. http://imf.org/external/data.htm

IMF Website. 2017. Direction of Trade Statistics. http://elibrary-data.imf.org/FindDataReports.aspx?d=33061&e=170921

Kmenta, J. 1997. *Elements of Econometrics: Second Edition.* Ann Arbor, MI: University of Michigan Press

Kennedy, P. 2008. *A Guide to Econometrics.* Hoboken, NJ: Wiley-Blackwell.

Patricia, E.G., and R.C. Kirkpatrick. 1994. *Time-Series Modelling and Forecasting in Business and Economics.* New York, NY: McGraw-Hill.

Pindyck, R., and D.L. Rubinfeld. 1998. *Econometric Models and Economic Forecasts.* New York, NY: Irwin/McGraw-Hill.

Ramanathan, R. 1998. *Introductory Econometrics with Applications.* Oak Brook, IL: The Dryden Press.

Verbeek, M. 2012. *A Guide to Modern Econometrics.* West Sussex, UK: Wiley and Sons.

Vu, T.B. 2015. *Seeing the Future: How to Build Basic Forecasting Models.* New York, NY: Business Expert Press.

White, H. 1980. "A Heteroskedasticity-Consistent Covariance Matrix Estimator and a Direct Test for Heteroskedasticity." *Econometrica* 48, no. 4, pp. 817–38.

Wooldridge, J.M. 2013. *Introductory Econometrics: a Modern Approach.* Scarborough, Canada: Nelson Education.

World Bank's World Development Indicators website. 2017. http://data.worldbank.org/data-catalog/world-development-indicators

About the Author

Tam Bang Vu is a Professor of Economics and Interim Dean of the College of Business and Economics at the University of Hawaii-Hilo. She has published more than 30 articles in refereed journals during the past ten years, including papers in renowned journals such as *Economics Letters, Applied Economics, Applied Economics Letters, Pacific Economic Review,* and *Journal of Asian Economics*.

Tam Vu has been teaching quantitative methods for ten years, including both Econometrics and Forecasting courses. Her classes are open to both undergraduate and graduate students with an interest in business and economics. She holds a PhD and a MA in Economics, a MM in Piano Performance, and two BAs in Fine Arts and Architecture. She is also a graduate cooperating faculty at the University of Hawaii-Manoa.

Index

www.ingramcontent.com/pod-product-compliance
Lightning Source LLC
Chambersburg PA
CBHW062029200326
41519CB00017B/4975